About the author

Jacqueline James was born in Birmingham and at the age of seven moved to the Cotswolds with her family. Her interest in the scientific basis of hand analysis began when she was reading for a degree in History; and the development of her techniques began during a long stay in Southern Spain shortly afterwards. She began practising professionally when her first child was born sixteen years ago. Her first book, *Take Control of Your Life*, was published in 1995.

Also by Jacqueline James

Take Control Of Your Life

Reinvent Your Life

Jacqueline James

Hodder & Stoughton

First published in Great Britain in 1996
by Hodder and Stoughton
A division of Hodder Headline PLC

10 9 8 7 6 5 4 3 2 1

A CIP catalogue record for this title is available from
the British Library.

ISBN 0 340 65431 7

Typeset by Palimpsest Book Production Limited,
Polmont, Stirlingshire
Printed and bound in Great Britain by
Cox and Wyman, Reading, Berkshire

Hodder and Stoughton
A division of Hodder Headline PLC
338 Euston Road
London NW1 3BH

Contents

1

Reinvent Your Life

Man's main task in life is to give birth to himself, to become what he potentially is.

(Erich Fromm)

Of all the billions of people in the world there is no one quite like you. There is no one who is going to have the same impact on the world as you, no one who is going to feel the way you do. You are unique, and the life you really want for yourself is the life you were, in fact, born to have. In your heart you know that, but as you go through each day with its demands and routines you probably feel that your life isn't turning out to be quite so special after all.

Well, this book is going to show you how to change that. It will not only show you how to become the person you were born to be; it will help you to reinvent your life.

Your body and brain contain everything you need to create and attract whatever you want in life: money, love, comfort, pleasure, creative fulfilment. You need no power outside yourself to attract and create all the circumstances that you want. You can achieve everything by the power of your thoughts. In fact, everything you have ever thought so far has brought you to where you are today. Your thoughts have created the life you lead, the money you have and your relationships.

Some of this may be just what you want. Some of it may not; and in this book I propose to show you how you have

arrived at your present position and how you can rework
the things you want to change so that your life is *exactly*
as you want it to be.

Some of you may already know that your thoughts also
create the lines on the palms of your hands and affect the
shape of your fingers. Each thought that arises in your mind
flows through your nervous system and is felt in every atom
and molecule of your body. In fact, medical science has
known for many years that neurological disturbances in
the brain affect the shape and direction of the lines on the
hand and can indicate future medical problems. Similarly,
research has shown that strongly held beliefs imprint the
patterns on your hands and these will dictate your future in
non-medical areas of your life. So, change your thoughts,
and the lines on your palms will change; and your life and
your future will change as well.

In this book we are going to take this idea much further,
so that you can get to the root of some of your beliefs. Most
of you are familiar with astrology and know under which
zodiac sign you were born. Many of you also know that
astrology is based on the position of the major planets when
we entered the world and drew our first breath of air.

What you may not know is that each of these planets is
represented on your hands. Each of your fingers corresponds
to a planet and will reflect the placing of that planet in
your horoscope. Each of the mounts in your palm also
corresponds to a planet. In other words, your astrological
horoscope is reflected in the shape of your fingers and hands
and the mounts on the palms. Furthermore, the way the lines
in your palm move towards or away from each mount is a
reflection of your horoscope at birth.

In my earlier book, *Take Control of Your Life*, I demon-
strated how your *conscious, everyday thinking* is constantly
affecting the quality, length and direction of your major
palm lines. In this book we are going to get to the
root of many of your *subconscious* thoughts – thoughts
created at birth and before conscious memory that have
been affecting your life without your awareness, but that

will also be reflected in the shapes of your hands, lines and mounts.

Again, as in *Take Control of Your Life*, we are going to turn 'prediction' on its head. With simple, enjoyable exercises you will discover how to reach those deep-rooted, subconscious influences, pull them to the surface and move yourself away from a 'destiny' that gives you a hard time. You will begin to have fun creating the life you really want.

First of all, let's take a look at how the major planets create an imprint on our psyches when we are born.

Just imagine it: there you are, cocooned for nine months in warm, amniotic fluid with all your needs met. You are floating in your own private sea, protected from the forces of gravity, and then, when you are fully developed, gentle contractions begin to unsettle your world. These become strong to the point of violence as you are forced out into a sudden barrage of sound and light. Cold air hits the surface of your skin and the umbilicus is cut. You are on your own. You either breathe or you die. That first breath becomes associated with survival, and our tiny bodies are now subject to the gravitational pull of the earth and all its orbiting planets. That first breath and the bombardment of planetary energy on our exposed bodies becomes imprinted on our barely formed minds and the planetary formations at that time are read by astrologers as our horoscope.

Many people think that the relationship between these planets at our birth has an absolute and permanent effect on our lives. They believe that by following the 'stars' they will discover their destiny. But the power of your inner will which translates itself into thought is stronger than any 'destined' pattern. Yes, I mean it. You are in control of your life. If it is not going the way you want it, your only mistake is to have accepted other blueprints for yourself. These have come from the planetary energies as outlined above, your genetic inheritance, your environment and ideas implanted by other people.

So if you feel dissatisfaction with any area of your life,

you can change it. In fact, you can go so far as to reinvent it, to clear your mind of past conditioning and recreate your whole lifestyle, finances and relationships.

Before you begin, however, Figure 1.1 will show you where the major planets are shown on your palm. Don't worry if it seems confusing. It doesn't matter if you know nothing at all about astrology. Your hands will show you what is happening, in the shape and the direction of the lines. Nor does it matter, at this stage, if you can't make head or tail of your hands either. All you need to know is how you feel about your life. This is your starting point.

Your dissatisfactions and frustrations will tell you what areas you want to work on and these will be reflected in your hands. As you work through the book you will get better at reading your hands and will notice the changes that will occur – maybe a more balanced finger or a stronger, longer line, and you will quickly see how these relate to the planets.

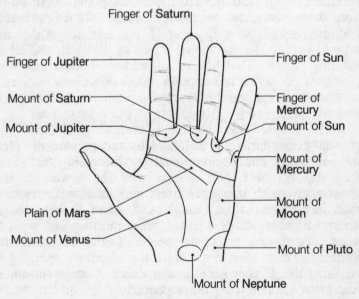

Figure 1.1

You don't need to get a horoscope done to follow the exercises in this book and to achieve the results you want. In fact, I feel that the quickest way to success is not to get bogged down with detail but to relax, enjoy the exercises and begin to treat yourself in a way that you probably have not done fully before.

All our relationships and the pressures to survive, to have a roof over our heads, food to eat, transport, holidays, etc., give us a certain outlook on life – a limited outlook. Throughout this book you will be shown:

- how the shapes of your fingers and mounts reveal your outlook and the way you react to events and people, thereby affecting your life;

- how to use enjoyable exercises to uproot the hidden thoughts and attitudes which have been subconsciously running your life;

- how to create a new blueprint for your life so that it flows easily towards happiness and fulfilling goals;

- how to attract the people and relationships that give you happiness;

- how to build an existing relationship into an even better one;

- how to build more prosperity and financial success;

- how to improve your health by recognising the planetary influences and enjoyably overcoming them.

Quite a few of you will be feeling, 'That's all very well, but I don't *know* what I want. All I know is that it ought to be something different from where I am now.'

So that is *your* starting point. You want something different.

You have already seen how the pull of gravity from all the planets can affect our newborn bodies and brains, but as tiny babies this process is reinforced as we absorb a way of looking at the world and life which is based on family and cultural attitudes. As this becomes ingrained, that spark which is unique to each one of us loses its voice. We forget who we really are. We forget the brilliance of our own life force and unique abilities as we struggle to cope with naming things, identifying things, making 'sense' of things. By the time we reach school if we haven't already half lost it, education organises our brains to overwhelm a good deal of whatever spark is left.

The reasoning qualities that education gives us are superb when in harness to this individual creative spark, but many of us experience problems because that spark has become dimmed almost to extinction. By following the exercises in this book you will begin to uncover it and to learn to use it.

You already have everything you need within you. All your frustrations, irritation, anger, apathy, failures are actually your true life force telling you that this is not what you want, not what you're supposed to be doing. Although most of us realise this, it can be tempting sometimes, either to give in, or to want to throw everything over and start afresh, only to find that we're beset with other problems.

The key, as you will find here, is to do it slowly and gently, uprooting unproductive and harmful ideas, uncovering the original spark, and building it more and more strongly into your life. You will begin to feel its effects in more enjoyment and a sense that each day is a pleasure and that your life is complete.

How This Works

Let's suppose that you're having difficulties, maybe at work, in your love life or in relationships in general. These will be shown in your hand.

For example, this may be because you have the planet Saturn placed in an unpromising position in your horoscope, indicating that your life is 'destined' to be fraught with difficulties. You probably won't know that Saturn is badly placed in your chart, but your finger of Saturn (see Figure 1.1) and lines of Saturn (explained in Chapter 9), will reveal the problem and you will experience it as frustration or delays and difficulties in getting what you want.

By working with specific exercises to deal with this, you will begin to notice changes in the lines on your hands. Your 'difficult' Saturn finger and its accompanying lines will begin to show balance and clarity and you begin to achieve easily what before seemed difficult or even impossible.

Of course, some of the planetary energies are superb and enhance our lives, so we naturally want to develop these. But we need to look at the whole picture of our lives and decide what planetary influences we want to enhance and which ones we want to overcome. They are all pictured on our hands. There is no major influence in our lives that does not appear there; so you have a map at every stage of your life to show you where you are and how you are doing.

In this book there is a chapter on each planet and the fingers or mounts to which it corresponds. At this stage, all you need to know is what areas of your life you want to improve. For example:

- Are your finances in a mess? Is this just occasionally or is it part of your life? Then you may want to concentrate on prosperity. It is possible to change yourself from poverty to wealth by reinventing your goals, your attitudes and approach.

- Is your love life causing you frustration or unhappiness? It is possible to turn this around too and have the happiness you want.

- Are you longing for success and recognition, either in your work or some project that is close to your heart? This can be turned round: many people, by working on the exercises in this book, have achieved success in ways they never dreamed of. It suddenly dropped into their lap when they had almost given up hope.

By steadily working through the exercises you will discover how to get exactly what *you* want in your life; what has been holding you back; and, above all, to realise that your old goals may no longer be what you truly want. By not achieving them in the past you may actually have become stuck on them. In this book you will begin to overcome anything you don't want or need, be in control and reinvent your life.

In the list that follows I have generalised some of the qualities of each planet so that you can see which area of your life you are concentrating on.

Sun	Success, money, creativity, achievement.
Moon	Intuition, love, family, weight.
Jupiter	Career, adventure, success, social life.
Venus	Love, culture, prosperity.
Mercury	Relationships, communication, creativity, work.
Mars	New beginnings, sex, power.
Saturn	Discipline, organisation, overcoming obstacles.
Pluto, Neptune & Uranus	Inspiration, rejuvenation, longevity, genius.

Certain qualities overlap in different planets: for example love is connected to Venus and the Moon; sex, which is related to love, is under Mars, and relationships are under Mercury. So, if your love life is the area you want to work on first, start with Venus, move on to Mercury and Mars; and the exercises for the Moon will help to fine-tune things. However, all the exercises will help to improve your life, so try to get round to each chapter and work with it when you can.

In most chapters you will find two levels of exercise. The most challenging are those that take you deeper into your innermost drives; it is often easier if they are put on a tape so that you can relax and enjoy the process. But many people also get excellent results working straight from the book.

In each chapter there are also many exercises that are lighter and simpler but just as effective. Generally, for the fastest results it is best to incorporate both, but your own intuition will tell you which ones to go for, and that will be the ideal programme for you.

You can do as much or as little as you like. The important thing is to enjoy it all and then just sit back: the results will come all by themselves, along with visible changes in the patterns on your hands.

2

Uncovering Your Inner Spark

Fear not that thy life shall come to an end, but rather
fear that it shall never have a beginning.

(Cardinal Newman)

Never mind horoscopes and planets for now. These represent
outside energies, and the most important thing in your life
is you. You are the centre of it. You are a mini-universe
in your own right. You contain within yourself absolutely
everything you need to live on planet earth, and I don't
mean just your senses so that you can see, hear, smell,
touch and taste. I also mean the magnetic power of your
brain to attract to itself everything it needs for your survival
and enjoyment: food and shelter; emotionally, love, sex and
friendship; creatively, money, work, play and so on.

Most of us are born into families that teach us how society
views these things. The environment in which we grow up is
also constantly affecting us, but at the core of every one of
us is something unique that wants to express itself in its own
way. It is this uniqueness that can get frustrated very early on
in our lives, and if you have been frustrated for too long you
begin to feel that this is what life is all about. Because your
thoughts create your future, continuing frustration *becomes
your future* when it was never meant to be.

What, you may say? Me? I'm a bricklayer or a nurse
or secretary. I'm OK. We can't all be rich or tycoons or
jet-setting or living the life of Riley.

Well, you'd be wrong. We can all be anything we want and if being a bricklayer or a secretary is what you want, that's fine. But we all change and you might have got stuck, or think that you're not capable of anything else. So don't sell yourself short.

The truth is that we all want different things and this deep, inner wanting is telling us what we are meant to be aiming for. It is telling us what our contribution to the world is meant to be. Yes, even wanting to be a millionaire. Millionaires usually create something pretty fantastic for the rest of us to enjoy. At the very least, they chivvy us up. You either like it or reject it like my friend, Anne, who was disgusted with the hedonism of a very wealthy mutual friend. She decided she wanted to live a simple life so she now lives somewhere warm (Spain) where the heating bills are less and she teaches yoga.

So who *are you* really? What would *make you happy*?

Uncovering Your Early Dreams

Step 1

This first exercise is the most fundamental and it is a good idea to do it when you can give yourself about an hour to go into it properly. This is time for *you*. This is time for you to begin to uncover who and what you really are and to nurture yourself.

Keep a piece of paper and pen beside you, sit down somewhere quietly and relax for a few minutes. Take a few deep breaths and stretch any area of your body that feels tense.

When you are ready, cast your mind back to your childhood, especially to that time somewhere between three and five. You may find this easier if you close your eyes. Some people find it difficult to imagine being three again but their intention to retrieve the memory is pulling on their memory banks and beginning to achieve results.

How did you see your world then? What particularly fascinated you? Did you love colour? Shapes? Sounds?

What fantasies and daydreams did you have then? Which ones did you act out in your games? Which ones did you keep secret? Ponder on this for a few moments. You may see it vividly or just get a hazy impression or feeling. Either way the exercise is working.

Most people had a rich fantasy life as a child, peopled with characters from stories, television or just made up. The way that these appealed to you and the way that you played with them is indicative of part of who you really are.

Now on your piece of paper write down the essence of those special dreams. You can make it into a full-blown account if you want to. But really dredge up those deep-seated dreams from the early memories of your life. Keep writing until you feel that you have done enough. This can be as little as one paragraph or as much as two sides of A4 paper.

So how do you feel? Is there anything in your current life that is the fruit of this? Or have you gone far away from it and feel a sense of loss or general frustration? Make a note of anything you feel is relevant for you now, anything that you feel you might like to develop in some way. Draw a circle round it or highlight it in a bright colour.

Emma's experience will show you how this can work.

Emma's Story

Emma is 28, lives in a small flat with her boyfriend and works as a personal assistant to the managing director of a company building specialised machines for biotechnology. Her lists looked like this.

My Life aged 3–5

I loved colour, especially reds, pinks, greens and blues with gold. Gold I loved especially. I loved its shininess whether it was metal or wrapping paper. I wanted to enter into it, enter into the colour, absorb it into myself. My special dreams involved secret places where I could hide. High green grasses, lying safely close to the ground. I wanted to be a fairy, to accomplish magic things, not to be subject to the things of the earth.

Step 2

For the next exercise – and it is related to the above – we are coming back to the present, to your fantasies right now.

Take another piece of paper and write at the top:

The Way I Would Like to Live

Write out in as much detail as possible what your life would be like. Be as fantastic and over the top as you like. We are aiming to reach the core of you, the very essence of what you want so that you can begin to work with it.

It is OK to be greedy. Many of us have been taught that the desire to be rich is morally wrong, that it is not the way to heaven, especially with all the poverty in the world. But in our society the most successful achievements are usually rewarded with money; so it is important to make sure that you are not sabotaging your own success and fulfilment by feeling that wealth is wrong. Wealth is a symbol of success; so if you want it, that's fine. Acknowledge it and go for it.

When your account feels complete, consider it carefully. Do you feel that anything in it is part of your life now? If not, either circle or highlight it. These are dreams that you still hold but *have not fulfilled*. Also circle those things that you want to develop more even if they do play a part in your life now.

Look carefully and ponder these highlighted or circled sections of both your lists. Do any ideas surface, any insights about yourself? Again, Emma's example will show you how this works.

Emma's Ideal Life

A large house which is kept clean by other people who don't get in my way. Freedom to come and go as I please. Plenty of money to travel about as I want, i.e. about double after tax of what I have now, which would be £25,000–30,000 per annum. Holidays abroad in beautiful places where I can think and feel free.

Freedom from restriction was the common factor on both lists, and on her childhood list she was surprised at the intensity of the memory of her love for colour and shiny things. Nothing of that quality was in her life at the time. Her flat was painted in Magnolia emulsion, the floor covering was of seagrass. Her clothes were nearly all neutral and black.

This was the first area she could change; so she went straight out to Tie Rack and bought three brightly coloured, inexpensive chiffon scarves. She said that she felt instantly better. She then set about redecorating her flat. Her boyfriend, who was in agreement, helped her. As she did so she began to feel a deep glow of new energy and excitement. Suddenly she knew that she didn't want to be a secretary any longer but was scared about insecurity (compare her childhood list and its love of secret, safe places). That fear was clearly marked in her hands by lots of worry lines leading up to her mount of Saturn and Saturn was in an awkward position in her horoscope (see Chapter 9).

Emma did many of the exercises that I shall be giving you and today runs her own stall at antique fairs. She pays great attention to the lights and colours for display, with the result that her stall looks like an Aladdin's cave of colours, precious and semiprecious gemstones and metals. She is also free to travel around and is currently working on her prosperity to achieve the financial aspects of her ideal life.

Step 3

Make your own blueprint. Take a piece of paper and at the top of it write:

My Blueprint

List the highlighted sections of both lists together with any new ideas about yourself and your life that may have emerged from doing the exercise.

This represents the first phase of uncovering what you really want and it is important that you do something straight away to get your new life started.

Maybe you felt an affinity with plants and animals? You could go out and buy a beautiful plant in a pot, or for your garden if you have one. A fascination with fitting things together? Go and get a model set, a tube of glue and make something. A love of helping your mother in the kitchen? Go and buy some yeast and flour, then make some bread and use all that effort required for kneading to re-energise your childhood self. Perhaps you longed to do grown-up writing as I did but didn't know how, so you filled the pages up with looped squiggles. Get a pad of paper and start writing down the first thing that comes into your head and let it keep on flowing until you run out of steam.

You may get a brilliant new idea just from doing this or you may feel frustrated or even irritated. Good. Frustration and irritation are trying to tell you something. This is the first shoot of the new you.

As you work through the book you will be developing this, creating further foundations for your life, and, above all, you will begin to see results, quite often dramatic ones. But before we get down to the specifics of your life and your hands, there is another important factor to be considered.

Left and Right Hands

The right hand is controlled by the logical, practical left brain and the left hand is controlled by the intuitive, imaginative right brain. In other words, your left hand represents your subconscious self and contains more of your inner dreams and potential than your right, which represents your normal everyday conscious self. This is reinforced by the majority of us choosing to use our right hands as the dominant one.

If you are left-handed you tend to be much more in touch with your intuitions and can be more sensitive to some of the forces at work in your life, being affected both positively and negatively.

However, there is another important factor of the right and left hands to be considered. Whichever hand you 'reject' to write with becomes slightly 'stuck' at the age of five, or whenever you learned to write. At that age, before the regimentation of school and the learning of pre-ordained ideas began to take effect, you were still in touch with your primal, unique self.

The following exercise will begin to put you back in touch with it.

Contacting the Power of the Hand You Don't Write With

Look at your blueprint and begin to frame some questions which would help you to achieve certain things on it. Using the hand you normally write with, write down the first question.

Now take the pen in your *other* hand, the hand you don't normally write with, and write down the first answer that comes into your head. Keep doing this with all your questions – write the question with your usual writing hand and write the answer with the other one.

The results will probably surprise you. Our non-writing hand is the one that has the childhood belief that most things are possible. The answers you get – although probably squiggly and practically illegible – will contain much more of your innate force before it became diverted by education and other people's beliefs in the ways of doing things.

To return to Emma, part of her question and answer was as follows:

Q. How can I receive double my income?

A. By working for it.

Q. How long would I have to work to achieve double my income?

A. Very little time if you change your attitudes.

Q. What changes do I have to make in my attitudes?

A. Know that you can have it. It can come in as little as three weeks.

Once she had started her antiques stall, this turned out to be very near the truth. She needed another £15,000 to double her salary and she received almost £12,000 from the sale of a series of Victorian paintings she had picked up at a house sale.

You can include questions about relationships here as well. Although at the age of three or so we tend to take emotional security for granted, it will almost certainly be part of your ideal environment now.

Keep your first blueprint handy; you may find it helpful to refer to it. As you work through the book you will be uncovering new and deeper aspects of yourself so that this initial blueprint will almost certainly develop and change. Furthermore, as you work on the techniques to achieve the aims of your blueprint, the patterns on your hands will also begin to change.

The length of time this takes depends on how much time you are putting into it and how deep your resistances are. However, as a general rule, as soon as you embark on *any* exercise some change is immediate. Money, for example, responds surprisingly quickly once clear goals have been set and I have known people to achieve a turnaround in as little as three to four weeks. More normally, however, considerable improvements take about six months to a year.

Relationships can take longer because we usually have so much emotion invested in them, but, even so, once you start to work on them you will see immediate improvements.

3

Wealth and Success:
Finger and Line of Sun

Those who have some means think that the most
important thing in the world is love. The poor know
that it is money.

(Gerald Brenan)

Your finger of Sun is the third or ring finger (see
Figure 3.1).

The relative shape, strength or weakness of this finger
will reflect the position of the Sun in your own horoscope
and its relationship to the position of the other planets at
your birth.

The Sun relates to the element of fire and rules Leo but
when you were born the Sun could have been in any one
of the twelve signs of the zodiac. There are very few of
us who don't know what sign this is and are fascinated to
learn the personality traits associated with this sign.

The Sun's energy relates very specifically to our birth –
some astrologers regard it as the entry point of our existence
– and by working with these energies within ourselves we
enhance our creativity and prosperity.

However, here we are concerned with the possible problems that may have been caused by the Sun's interaction
with the planets at your birth. You don't need to know
exactly what these are unless you are keen to get a full
horoscope done. Your own fingers of Sun on right and

left hands will tell you all you need to know to begin to get your life the way you want it.

The ideal shape for your finger of Sun is for it to be balanced along all three phalanges. These are the divisions of the finger – the first being from the nail to the first joint, the second from first to second joint, and the third from the second joint to the knuckle. If any one of these phalanges is shorter, thinner or fatter than the others it indicates some area of your life that can be worked on profitably.

There is a kind of arrogance and recklessness about a full and well-balanced finger of Sun that is longer than the finger of Jupiter (see Figure 3.2). It represents an enormous belief in oneself and the power of divine providence. If this is supported by solidity in other areas of the palm – a well-balanced finger of Saturn, for example (see Chapter 9) – it can reveal someone who is going to be very successful, especially in the arts and finance. This can be seen on the

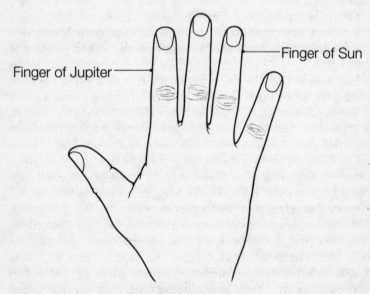

Finger of Sun

Finger of Jupiter

Figure 3.1

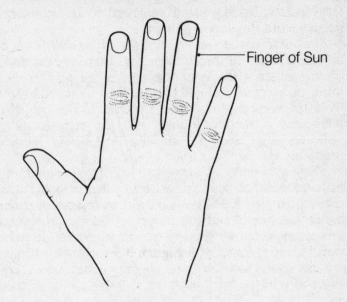

Finger of Sun

Figure 3.2

hands of several famous film stars and also tycoons. So if you have a comparatively long finger of Sun it means that you are well on the way to achievement, provided it is built on solid foundations.

To do this you will need to work to build up your finger of Jupiter as well (see Chapter 5), as balance between these two fingers will create more harmony in your achievement. The exercises later will help you with this.

If the first two phalanges of your finger of Sun are long and full, money-making can almost become an art form. You have a Midas touch, and it has been my experience that everyone who works on prosperity with the techniques I shall be giving you, tends to fill out on these two phalanges.

The reverse of this Midas touch is to have the phalanges short or wasp-waisted; so these techniques will help to fill this out as well (see Figure 3.3).

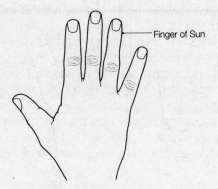

Figure 3.3

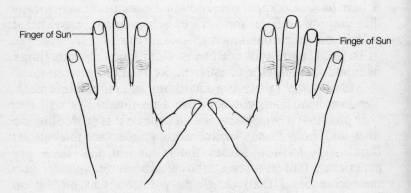

Figure 3.4

Problems on the Sun finger are also revealed if it is much shorter than the finger of Jupiter. If yours is like this it means that you believe that you have to work hard for everything you get and can sometimes step back so that others get ahead at your expense.

If your finger of Sun is long and full on the left hand and shorter or weaker on the right (Figure 3.4) it means that you have an innate ability to do well with money and the arts but have not fulfilled this quality in your life.

If the position is reversed – shorter or weaker on the left and longer and fuller on the right – it means that you were born with difficulties but have overcome them to achieve a measure of success or prosperity. However, there will always be a niggling anxiety because of the weaker left finger and this could still trip you up until you have worked on the beliefs and energies that have caused it.

Another important factor of the Sun's energy as it is revealed in your hand is *the line of Sun*.

This rises on the mount of Sun just beneath the Sun finger and travels down the palm (see Figure 1.1 on p.4 and Figure 3.5). The point where it meets the lifeline is the stage in life where you can expect some important success. Time on the lifeline is measured from its beginning between the thumb and index finger upwards across the palm. On average one centimetre represents ten years but if your hand is large, increase this slightly; if it is small, decrease it.

But if you can't find a nice long line, if it stops at the heart or head line, don't worry. These exercises will help you to create a brand new line, and once it is there it means that your brain has absorbed all the necessary information and energy to bring success into your life.

In other words, no matter what sabotage may have been caused in your life by the planetary positions at your birth, you can change it for the better. In fact, in time you can practically wipe out your early problems so that your life is completely transformed. Most of the major life reversals that I have seen have taken between one and seven years,

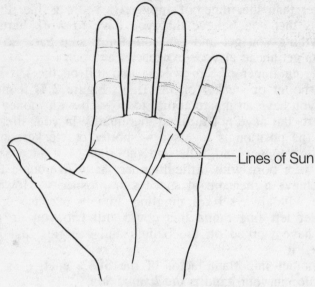

Lines of Sun

Figure 3.5

depending on the intensity of effort. For a seven-year turnaround some people have left off the techniques for months at a time, probably only working on them for a week or two occasionally. So it is up to you. However little you do, you will achieve something.

Increasing Your Own Success and Prosperity

There are very few of us who don't have some subconscious sabotage mechanisms in operation where money is concerned. We may have a good finger of Sun but will still get sidetracked by doubt, lack of confidence, or even a kind of self-destruct mechanism that comes into operation as we are nearing success. Certain key phrases are often part of our habitual thinking. There is the *spend mentality*—

- If I've got it I'll spend it.
- I might be dead next year so I'm going to live for the moment.
- Oh come on, let's blow the lot and party.
- I want it so I'm having it now on my Visa card.

Or the *poverty mentality*—

- Money doesn't grow on trees.
- Hard work never killed anyone.
- I can't leave this job (paying a pittance).
- I don't want the hassle of a high-paying job.
- You only get to the top if you work eighteen hours a day.
- Women don't make much money.

In the following exercise we are going to take a guided visualisation to uncover some of the roots of these ideas. You may find it helpful to tape this or get a friend to read it to you.

Uncovering the Source of Your Money Ideas

Remember the first exercise, when you were aged three to five. Sit quietly now, close your eyes and return to that time. As with the first exercise, don't be concerned if it seems hazy. Your intention will uncover what you need to know. Go back to your earliest memory of your family all sitting down together – maybe at a mealtime or a time when you were playing and your parents were nearby. If you were in a children's home then, see yourself with the other children and your carers at mealtimes.

Now try to remember what was said about money. Try

to remember what image you had of money, work and achievement. Was one parent or both parents working? Allow yourself to drift back to any feelings or ideas, however disjointed and disconnected they may seem. What ideas about life and money did you pick up from their conversation? Did you perceive your parents as success-ful? Maybe your grandparents or another adult had a big influence on your thoughts. Recall this now.

Feel the atmosphere. What was the décor like? At mealtimes were you in a high chair or sitting at the table? Was someone feeding you? Did you feel secure or was someone forcing you to eat? What was the food like?

Allow your thoughts to drift and recall how your feelings here affected your ideas about grown-up life, about work. Did life seem a good prospect or difficult? What did you take on board here that is still with you?

Continue with this reverie until you feel that you have completed it.

Now take a piece of paper and at the top write:

Earliest Ideas Absorbed About Success and Money

List all the ideas that have emerged from the preceding exercise.

The first thing you must realise is that these ideas are man-made. They are ideas held by other people that have been handed down to you. You are an adult now and in a position to choose; so we will take a look at some of the choices you made just a little bit later.

Take another piece of paper and at the top write:

My Ideal Future Aged 12–15

Now before you begin to write, sit down, close your eyes, take yourself back to this time of adolescence and recall the dreams you had then. How did the future seem to you? Bright? Full of opportunity? Something on which you were going to make your mark? What did you want to do with it? Were you going to have adventures? Become a big shot in business? Be a pilot? An air hostess? Really get down to the feelings you had then. They are still there, stored in your memory banks.

What things did you have then that gave you pleasure? A special penknife? Pencil-case? Hairbrush? Watch? Nail varnish? See them and remember what sort of feeling they gave you and what you wanted to do with them.

When you have done enough, take up your pen and paper and write down all your dreams.

Now close your eyes again and *imagine how you would have liked your life to be if you could turn the clock back*, and what you would have done differently. With hindsight, did you screw yourself up by your own attitudes? If so, change these in your mind's eye. What you are doing here is fusing the old desires with those that came later from experience, ideas perhaps of breaking out of a mould that is stifling you because you know that your earlier dreams have gone off the rails.

Allow the ideas to blend until you have come up with what may be a newer version of your adolescent ideas. Write down anything new or a different way of doing something.

Compare the two lists:

1. ideas absorbed aged 3–5;

2. your new blueprint which contains your modified adolescent dreams.

There are probably some discrepancies between 1 and 2.

Maybe you've absorbed the idea that security depends on working hard and yet you want to laze around on a beach for three months of the year. You've absorbed the idea that women don't make much money, yet you are a woman and you want to be rich.

The truth is that if you continue with your negative ideas you will never get truly what you want.

So let's change it.

Step 1

Take your blueprint and lists and think about them. Can any of your dreams be fitted into your life immediately? Or are you tied down with problems?

See what the essence of these dreams is. For example, Julie, aged 32 and with a husband, children and mortgage, had a list like this:

Aged 12 I wanted a flat in London, a Jaguar, to wear my hair long and blonde and be ultra-sophisticated with a brilliant job that pays you lots of money. Business trips to Paris and New York. Wonderful clothes. A boyfriend or lots of them. Bags of romance.

This is light years from her current position but the essence of it is glamour and the freedom that plenty of money can bring. The glamour she can introduce now. She can have her hair dyed and restyled as she likes. She can update her wardrobe and completely revamp her image. The money we can deal with in this chapter. The boyfriends we will deal with in Chapter 6, under Venus.

Step 2

Make a list of everything that seems beyond your grasp from your blueprint.

Step 3

Go back to your list of absorbed ideas and try writing each one with your non-dominant hand: the left if you are a right-handed person, the right if you are a left-handed person. It will slow you down and the feelings that come up may be very different from what you expect.

For example, one of my absorbed ideas was: 'Hard work never killed anyone.'

When I write it out with my right hand I am reminded

constantly of hearing it from my father, a successful man. My feelings are those of love and respect for him and a belief that this is how one becomes rich and successful.

When I write it out with my left hand I am like a child looking at it, and when I get to the word 'killed' it seems a totally alien concept. But with my left hand I realise that my feelings of total trust and acceptance of this belief are as alive as ever; and yet my adult self rejects them. They are not my ideas and I no longer want them.

Make a note of any feelings you have, whether they are of resistance or surprise, as you work your way down your list.

Step 4

Using your non-dominant hand, turn each negative absorbed idea into its opposite. Mine would now be something like: 'Hard work can be fun', or 'Hard work can be fun and profitable', or 'I am a success whether I work hard or not'.

If you can manage it, try to write each reversed statement out several times with your non-dominant hand. I know it's hard and I know that you can barely read it and that is *precisely* why the exercise is effective: you are using a dormant part of your psyche and teaching it a new way of looking at life.

Step 5

Using your blueprint and lists, write positive statements about the things you want on there. When you do this it is important to write affirmative statements including your first name, and always use the present tense. Psychologists have found that this is the most effective way to give your brain the kick-start it needs to get results.

Julie's list looked like this.

1. I, Julie, can now have a lovely car.

2. I, Julie, am attracting a lovely car.

3. I, Julie, am now building towards an interesting new career.

4. I, Julie, am able to take trips to Paris or New York anyway.

Add any other things that have become part of your dreams as an adult. You may even find that some of your dreams have become obsolete for you; so take these out.

Now write them all out, one by one, with your non-dominant hand and make a note of any new thoughts or anxieties or inspirations that come up.

Also Put in the amount of money you feel you need to accomplish this. It's OK to come out in a cold sweat as you write £50,000 or £250,000 or whatever. The cold sweat or the snigger of scorn is telling you that you have something to work on. It is your entry point to the place where you make it happen: your brain, your nervous system, your cellular structure, in short the whole you. Every part of you carries an imprint of your conditioning and as long as the imprint remains, your brain and body will make sure that it is brought into being.

So you are going to change it. You are going to get what you have always wanted; and you are going to do what you were born to do. You don't believe me? Try it and see.

Power Building

Because the body and brain are a complete unit you are going to use both to create what you want.

These techniques are similar to those used by athletes to enhance performance. You are going to choose some simple exercise that you currently find a bit difficult to perform. Press-ups, for example. If I try to do press-ups I manage about five before I think I'm going to expire. With the following exercise the aim is to increase by a small amount the number you can *easily* do. You will use visualisation and link this with your life goals so that improvement is naturally accepted by the brain.

So, first of all choose some small exercise that you can comfortably perform. It could be sit-ups or bicycling with your legs in the air. Or you could use yoga postures. With these you visualise yourself stretching that bit further into a perfect position.

Do your chosen exercise now to see how many you can perform – or with yoga see how far you can stretch comfortably. Above all, don't strain. As soon as you feel the slightest bit uncomfortable – even if you've only done two that's fine – stop.

And if at this moment you are inwardly groaning and planning to skip to the next section, *don't*. The example of a housewife from Swindon should convince you that your mind is stronger than matter. You may have read about it in the papers a few years ago. This woman lifted a three-quarter-ton Nissan truck to release her nine-year-old son who was trapped beneath it. Three quarters of a ton! We're not talking about a human weight of a few stone. We're talking about the weight of twelve people of ten stone each. She was only 5 foot 2 inches and weighed nine and a half stone and she says that her mind went blank. Her *only thought* was to save her son.

Imagine what you could do with that kind of single-minded determination. Of course, we don't want a life and death drama to activate that mind-over-matter power so we are going to build it steadily and naturally.

So you have chosen the exercise you want to perform and you know that you are not brilliant at it. Choose also the amount of money you would like to make your dream life possible. I find this works best if you select a mega sum and see that as your overall aim, but scale it down to make these first attempts more realistic – for realistic is what they become. For example, if you think £500,000 would make your life the way you really want it and you have £500 in the bank, first of all select a percentage of the £500,000, say £5,000, and work with that until your confidence grows. You can then upgrade it to £50,000 and so on.

Visualisation

Sit down somewhere comfortable and close your eyes. Take ten deep breaths, drawing the air deep into your lungs and letting it out again so that your abdomen rises and falls. Then visualise your chosen exercise and see yourself performing it perfectly. Feel the energy that courses through your perfect body so that it functions at optimum level. See the number of press-ups, etc. that you want to accomplish after your initial attempt. If you could only do two or three, see yourself doing between six and ten. Visualise the actual figure.

Now slowly open your eyes and stand up. When you feel ready, perform your chosen exercise as many times as is comfortable.

There, did you surprise yourself? If you didn't, you're cheating and telling yourself it's all rubbish and that amounts to the same verification: thought produces results.

Now sit down again, close your eyes and gently introduce the amount of money you want to achieve, say £5,000. Imagine what £5,000 looks like. See yourself going to the bank to get it out.

Your body and brain have just learned that they can produce physical results by visualising them, so you are going to reinforce this around money too. Go to your wallet or purse and take out a £10 note (and if you don't have one, get one for next time). Sit down with the note, place it on a piece of writing paper and by the side of it write:

$$£10 \times 500 = £5,000$$

If you're feeling flush and have the time, you can get £100 out of the bank and follow the same procedure:

$$£100 \times 50 = £5,000$$

Your mind has shown you that your body can deliver results with visualisation. It can do the same with money.

After a while you can dispense with the physical parts of this exercise if you want to and just visualise for the life you want. But if you ever feel stuck, you can include the physical exercise again for a bit of revision.

Results

I first started using these techniques in 1989 when I seemed to be bogged down with a great deal of work and very little financial return. A friend had invited me to a prosperity workshop, where I was asked to state what amount of money I needed to make my life easier. At first I was diffident, as I expect you will be. 'Oh, I just need a bit more each week.'

'How much more and what for?' came the answer 'Are you satisfied with that? For God's sake, this is your life. Is that the best you can come up with?'

They were right. They gently bullied me off my moral high ground of 'I work so hard. Aren't I virtuous? Just look what a good girl I am,' until I saw that I really wanted a good life and to get it I needed to make some big changes.

Those big changes are the same as yours will be: *think bigger and go for it*. Don't sit around hoping things will get better. Decide:

(a) what amount of money you need;

(b) when you need it by;

(c) what you're going to do with it when you've got it.

Then write affirmations of what you want in the present tense.

If you're like me, to begin with you might despair of ever being successful with money. That despair is all your negative thinking coming up, but if you persist in the techniques it will pass.

Within days of the workshop I began to get really bright and effective ideas to increase my finances, and throughout 1989 my finances increased in leaps and bounds in ways that would never have occurred but for these techniques.

Today, seven years later, my finances have gone from strength to strength. I have studied investments and organised the money I have made so that I don't have to work at all if I don't want to. Seven years ago such an idea would have sounded impossible to me and probably sounds preposterous to you now.

But the fact is that you *can* have anything you want. All you have to do is to decide just what that is, practise these techniques either often or occasionally and you *will definitely* get there sooner or later – sooner if you really go for it, later if you dabble. But if dabbling is how you like to do it, then that's fine.

The following two stories will give you further examples of the process.

Jenny's memories aged 3–5

Jenny's father owned a newsagent's, sweetshop and grocer's and they lived at the back of the shop. She remembers sitting in a high chair at the table with her mother trying to feed her. Jenny's lips were sealed tight. She had already decided that she hated her mother because force was used for everything Jenny either didn't want to do or didn't understand. Her attention was focused on her father, whom she saw working hard in the shop, being much respected by the assistants and liked by the customers. Jenny saw that work was something that could be a fun, jokey, friendly thing.

On a Sunday morning, her father would add up the accounts and money for the week. He would do this on the dining table with a close friend to help and they would both be drinking a pint of beer each. She saw the money being counted out into piles and began to associate the accumulation of money not only with food but also with an enjoyable time with a friend.

On a Sunday afternoon her father would drive the family into the country where they would walk or play games and always have an ice-cream or sweets. Money again became associated with treats. Her mother was only a vague figure in all this and Jenny remembers deciding that she did not want to be like her. She wanted the action and fun of her father's life.

This was reinforced as she got older, when her father left the shop and opened a warehouse importing dried fruits and spices. This grew into a considerable import business. They moved to a large house with hired help and Jenny saw her mother spending most of her days reading or shopping.

Jenny's list of absorbed ideas

1. Work is fun.

2. Money is easy to make.

3. Money creates a nice life.

4. Women don't work.

5. Women don't make money.

6. I'm not going to be like my mother.

Today, numbers 4 and 5 on Jenny's list would not apply in many households, but for anyone born before 1960 their experience would often have been of a mother at home.

Jenny's adolescent dream list

1. Spend all day every day riding my own pony.

2. Live in a lovely old cottage with an open fireplace where I entertain fellow riders to meals.

3. Have my hair done every week and go to smart parties.

Before Jenny did these techniques she went to college and then into advertising where she thought she would find the excitement, money and glamour she wanted. But reality didn't match her expectations. After doing these techniques she decided to follow her dream. She now owns a small riding school where she breeds competition horses.

Jenny was very fortunate because her father gave her an ongoing picture of business success and that filled her mind with the idea that she could do it too.

Compare this with Rob, Jenny's partner, whose father worked for a local farmer. When he was a child they lived in a cottage tied to the farm and this home was, therefore, dependent on Rob's father continuing to work there.

Rob's memories aged 3–5

'My first memories are of sitting at the table with the sunlight coming in at the window, a large jug of fresh creamy milk from the farm on the table and my mother fretting about my father's filthy clothes. They argued a lot about the hours he worked – up at 5 a.m. all seasons and weathers and not back before 7 p.m. He rarely ate with us because as kids we couldn't wait until seven. Often we were in bed before he got back home.

'We were in awe of his boss – a posh bloke with blond hair and talking as if he had ten plums in his mouth – and Mum drilled us to be polite to him because the house and job depended on it.

'When I was nine we were forced to leave the cottage. The farmer wanted to sell it and my father couldn't afford the rent of anything else. I remember my mother crying a lot and when my father got a job in a factory in town she went round and told the farmer what she thought of him.

'But it made me feel inferior. I was aware that there were people out there who could control me and ruin me if they wanted.

'The factory was actually much better for us. Dad worked better hours and earned more money. Our standard of living went up but now I can see that it gave me the idea that I'd be safe only if I worked in a factory and yet I longed to be in the country.'

Rob's list of absorbed ideas

1. You have to work long and hard to make a pittance.

2. Security depends on working hard.

3. There are rich and powerful people who can ruin me.

4. Other people are stronger than I am.

5. You can never say what you feel in case other people ruin you.

6. Your life is not your own.

7. You can only make enough money for your basic needs.

8. Rich people are in a world apart – I can never be one of them.

Rob's adolescent dream list

To make enough money to go back and make Captain Smith grovel [the farmer who had turned them out of their home and not his real name].

That was all that was on it. Rob could see no further.

He tried working in a factory, but hated it. He longed to be back in the country, so he then got a job working with horses and became an excellent rider. It wasn't until he met Jenny, though, that his life began to take off. They met just after Jenny had bought her yard and had also bought a mare for breeding that had come from Rob's employers.

They became friends and eventually lovers, with Rob moving in and taking over the training of the competition horses. Rob did achieve his adolescent dream when he entered several local horse shows. Captain Smith's children, now grown-up, who were around the same age as Jenny and Rob, also often competed and Rob described the first time that he actually won a local trophy, beating them hands down, as the most delicious of his life. It was also a great healing, and he felt free to set new goals for success in his life.

Jenny's finger of Sun was strong. She had her Sun in Aries, which made her fiery and adventurous, so she had a double dose of help from both her horoscope and her environment. Rob was the opposite. His finger of Sun was weak. His Sun was in Taurus, giving strength on the earthy side, but both his palm and his horoscope showed that fire and enthusiasm were lacking and his early life reinforced this. His finger of Sun has since filled out and balanced up. He and Jenny formed a company and are very prosperous.

Your situation may not be so extreme, but whatever it is you can enhance the positive qualities as Jenny did or overcome them, like Rob.

Magnetising

'Fate' is magnetic. It is created by your thoughts. Every thought you think causes electromagnetic currents to emanate from it. These waves are going out from you and, just as radio waves can transmit precise sound and images across the ether, so will your brain waves. Out there somewhere is a receiver of your images – animate or inanimate.

Most of the time our thoughts are a jumble: they go

round and round in our heads and simply create a jumbled energy in our immediate vicinity. We all know when a friend or colleague is feeling off. Apart from verbal signals like grumbling or anger, we also sense it physically.

But as soon as your thoughts become focused they have clarity and power and will not only travel further but will create results much more quickly.

This next exercise is an extension of the visualisation from power building and you may like to put it on tape.

Magnetising exercise

Sit down somewhere quietly and close your eyes. Take a few deep, calming breaths and relax a little more fully. As you do so, allow the image to come of the things you really want. Let's suppose it was, like me a few years ago, to release your workload and have a freer life: see yourself leading that freer life. What are you doing? Shopping? Going to college? Lying on a beach? Partying with friends? Travelling?

Really get into the images. Is the sun shining? Is there a slight breeze? How do these things feel against your skin? What sort of smells are there? Garlic and black tobacco in a hot country, for example. Bad drains. Heavy perfumes.

How do you feel and look? Full of life and vitality? What are you wearing? Have you changed your image? If so, how does it make you feel? Do you want to make any adjustments to this? If so, do it now.

Perhaps you want a successful career. See yourself in the surroundings that such success would bring – the smart office, the meetings, the travel, the company car or whatever qualities your particular success story would bring.

Perhaps your image is of a new lover. See the pair of you together leading the kind of life you really want with a lover. You can make this as romantic or fantastic as you like. You are in the process of creating what you really want. Realise that now you have visualised it something has been activated. Not just in your brain but the electromagnetic currents that emanate from it. Because your images are focused they will be drawn to any like energy.

Another person, for example, who is 'on the same wavelength' as you, who is looking for new love, can pick up these energies at a subconscious level and the two of you will be activated towards each other. Maybe several people will cross your path because of it. Rest assured that what you give out, you will ultimately receive.

Similarly with lifestyle. If your brain is transmitting freedom and exotic climes, that will be registered, and opportunities to make the change will come into your life.

The same is true of money. Imagine this coming to you in a variety of ways – through your letterbox in the form of a cheque perhaps, a win on the lottery or pools, a pay rise, an extra sum of money for work you've done, a gift.

Another important factor here is how you feel as you see your dreams coming closer in your visualisation. There you are, for example, visualising a new love and seeing that person coming closer into your life. Do you love the prospect? Or does it make you feel uncomfortable? If you feel worried or guilty you need to work on this. It is blocking you. Just look carefully at it. Perhaps your aims are going to hurt someone you love. Maybe you're in a stale relationship and want new excitement. We'll go into this more fully in Chapter 6. For now, just be aware of it.

Magnetising can be used for small things as well. For example, for three years I had to take my children along the Oxford ring road in the rush hour every day. On wet winter evenings, entering the dual carriageway from the slip road was treacherous and there were many accidents, so I 'created a space' for my car.

I did *one* magnetising session where I visualised a space for my car, clearly seeing myself driving down the slip road with any cars in front of me also easily finding space in the flow so that I wasn't snarled up behind them.

Every time I got into the car to make the journey, I mentally repeated the affirmation: 'A perfect space is being created for me in the traffic flow.' The result was that, without fail, when I went down that slip road in my car, despite the traffic being nose to tail at 60–70+ m.p.h., there was always a gap. And every time I drove into it I said thank you, not out of some half-baked piety but because I really was glad that my journey was being made easier.

The only time it didn't work was when I was forced to use my husband's GTi one wet, dark evening. His wing mirrors were in a slightly different place, the acceleration was like a rocket and I began to get agitated. That agitation had me stuck on the slip road for several minutes waiting for a space, with other cars backing up the slip road behind me, blowing their horns and flashing their lights.

Research done by the police both with aerial-view heli-copters and ground crews interviewing the victims of accidents have said that nearly all snarl-ups and accidents are caused by people who are emotionally upset. Complete bottlenecks but with no accident are often caused by someone who has had a row with a partner or colleague just before the journey.

So by making affirmations like mine you are calming yourself and the energy around you.

Clearing Your Mind of Obstacles

If, during your magnetising exercise, you had feelings of guilt or doubt, that something wasn't quite right, or simply that you didn't think you would succeed, it is essential to root these feelings out.

With money, for example, you are quite likely to feel that the sum you want is too great. One of the best ways to countermand this is to make affirmations. These begin to fill your mind with ideas of success and to overwhelm the negative statements your mind has grown used to.

For example (always remember to insert your first name):

I (your name) am now able to increase my wealth by the power of my thoughts.

It is OK for me————to have what I want.

Creating what I————want is making me happier and also everyone around me.

If you were feeling anxious or guilty about asking for new love, is this:

(a) because you are already in a relationship and don't know what to do?

(b) because you don't feel lovable enough or attractive enough?

For (a) you need to take small steps towards what you want, all the while examining your reasons for wanting change. The relationship may be near its end and these exercises will help you forwards. Or it may simply need an overhaul, in which case these exercises will reveal that and you can work on Chapters 6 and 7 to improve it.

For (b) use affirmations to build up your self-esteem. For example:

I————now accept that I am lovable.

Wonderful new people now see how desirable I am.

I————find love and happiness wherever I go.

You will soon get the idea and can make up affirmations to suit your particular circumstances.

Charging Up Your Own Sun Energy

This is going to sound obvious but the fact is that most of us don't do it. The Sun is a fire energy and if your own resources are depleted you simply need to get near fire.

In the summer it is easy. After protecting your skin, you simply get out into the sunshine. In the winter if you have an open fire just sit or lie in front of it and notice how it raises your energy levels.

Another excellent way of boosting energy levels is by burning candles. One will do, but five or six are better if you are feeling low. I also find that it helps for people who have a lot of brainwork to do to have one burning on their desk or table. Obviously in an office this is not practical but if you are working at home it can help to keep you going cheerfully for quite a bit longer.

Alternatively, you could use an aromatherapy burner, which is a ceramic container for a small candle and essential oils. These are inexpensive and can be bought from most candle shops or from Culpeper's (address on page 213). Good aromatherapy oils to burn are lavender and lemon, which are generally therapeutic, rejuvenative, uplifting and smell lovely.

Candle shops are becoming big business, so you have plenty to choose from.

Achieving Results

To see these coming in fairly quickly you need to do all four processes regularly:

(a) affirmations

(b) power building

(c) visualisation

(d) magnetising

A suggested way of working would be to write your affirmations five times each for ten days with both right and left hands.

Power building can be done three or four times a week for a month.

Magnetising or visualisation can take over from power

building after a month and be done once or twice a week along with occasional affirmations until you begin to see results. Most people start to notice changes within the first few weeks.

As soon as these changes begin to take place in your life you will notice changes on your hands. The phalanges (the three segments of the fingers) will start to balance out, becoming fuller if they were thin-looking, and you may notice a deepening of some lines or new branch lines. These line changes are different for each person, but as you work through the book you will begin to see their significance.

4

Intuition and Creativity: The Moon

I felt a rare rush of luxuriant delight. Everything lay before me, and all I had to do was receive it.

(Jane Smiley)

Most of us are aware of the influence of the Moon in our lives. It controls the tides, raising and releasing the seas and oceans. If it can pull oceans, we know that it can also affect our own bodies which are at least 70 per cent water. The full moon is renowned throughout folklore for its effect on werewolves and the mentally disturbed. It is also on record that more crimes are committed at this time.

The Moon is associated with the feminine side of our nature: the receptive, the passive. This aspect contains our dreams and our nightmares, our fears and anxieties. Expressed like this, it can seem that it corresponds to our weakness, but in fact it is the essential place to start if we are to reinvent our lives, counterbalancing the active, more masculine aspects of the Sun. It is fertile ground linked with our primitive, childish self that is frightened of the dark and the dangers that may lurk there. It is the untamed part of us before civilisation began to deny its power. It is where our intuition resides and the imaginative dreams which, if acted upon, can propel us to achieve things that have never been done before. In other words, when you use the power of the Moon in your own psyche, you overcome weakness and fear.

Some of you will know quite a bit about the Moon, especially if you are born under the zodiac sign of Cancer, which is ruled by it.

When each one of us was born the Moon was in a particular position of the zodiac in relation to the other planets. As a result, in some people it will have a strong influence and in others a weak one. Your hands will reveal this for you and you can begin to work on the techniques in this chapter so that instead of being at the mercy of the Moon's position at your birth you can use it as a tool. In doing this, you become powerful as you were meant to be and lead your life as *you* want it.

On the hands the mount of Moon is positioned on the cusp, as in Figure 4.1.

A fleshy, full mount here denotes someone who is imaginative and intuitive. If there is also a girdle of Venus beneath the middle two fingers it means that you are extremely sensitive, often imagining problems or slights when there are few or none at all.

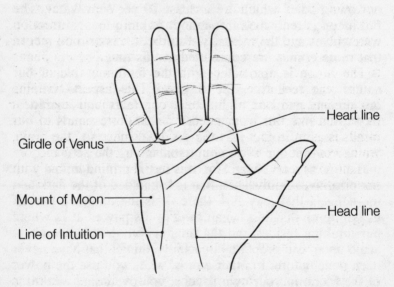

Figure 4.1

But it is fairly simple to harness this sensitivity to serve you so that you continue to see all the possibilities in a situation, relationship or personality without becoming so emotionally involved. When this happens you can see further than most and it is an excellent tool to use at work and in your personal life, leading you away from trouble into creativity.

If you have a line of intuition as well, which spans the mount of Moon, it means that you are relatively psychic and will definitely see and understand more than most. In your birth horoscope you would probably have the Moon in a water sign like Pisces, Cancer or Scorpio and also you would probably have an important planet in Scorpio, such as the Sun or Mars, or have Scorpio in the ascendant.

For our purposes here, it does not matter whether you know any of this: your hand will tell you all you need to know.

If your mount of Moon has a flattened appearance, it means that as yet your intuitive nature is lying dormant or not being used as much as it could be. We all have the capacity to develop our intuitions and sixth sense. Indeed, it *was* much more developed in our ancestors and only began to diminish as we moved into the industrial age and began to use our reasoning power to achieve what we wanted.

The reasoning aspect of our minds is associated with the left hemisphere of the brain, which controls the development of the lines on our *right* hand. The intuitive aspect of our minds is associated with the *right* hemisphere of the brain, which controls the formation of lines on our *left* hand.

You have two things to consider for reinventing your imaginative, intuitive life:

(a) Is the mount of Moon fleshy or flat?

(b) Is it different on right and left hands?

If it is developed, and perhaps with a line of intuition on the *left* hand but not so clear on the *right*, it means that you are already potentially gifted with a sixth sense but have suppressed it.

If it is the other way round – full on the *right* with perhaps a line of intuition, but flattened on the *left* with a feathery or non-existent line of intuition – it means that you *want* to develop your sixth sense and are working towards it, but the flattened left mount of Moon is warning you that it is not yet balanced in you. In other words, your perceptions may not always be accurate and could lead you astray.

Whatever the aspects of the Moon on your hands, the exercises that follow are designed to help you to develop your intuitive faculties more fully so that you can live your life the natural way in which it was meant to be lived, with a harmonious flow between your intuition and your actions. The result of this is more success, comfort, prosperity and joy. The mount and lines will change to reflect this.

Although it can sometimes take several months or so before you see changes on your mount of Moon, benefits begin to occur from the very first exercise. You are simply uncovering the real you.

Uncovering Your Deepest Impulses

In the earlier exercises, where you looked at the life you wanted aged about three and in early adolescence, you were using your conscious mind. Now you are going to be taken back to the time before conscious memory. Unless you have already done some rebirthing or deep work on your psyche, this may be the first time that you have taken a look at this. It is probably the most important unexplored area of your mind because in it are contained the essence and spark of your individuality. Because it is the time when our conscious memories were not sufficiently formed we tend to regard it as mysterious, but we do have a subconscious memory of it and this is what you are going to contact now. It is simple, safe and can do you no harm. However, it can sometimes uncover emotions that you are suppressing, so if it begins to feel at all uncomfortable, stop. You may want to explore these feelings a little or you may prefer to leave them alone for the time being. If so, make a note of them so that you can work on them later. Generally, most people enjoy recognising these suppressed feelings and feel a sense of release.

Exercise for uncovering your deepest impulses

You will need a quiet room and an uninterrupted twenty minutes or so. You may find it helpful to record this on a cassette tape.

Sit or lie down and make sure that you are warm. If not, cover yourself with something like a blanket or sleeping bag and relax quietly for a few minutes, breathing deeply. Taking more oxygen into your lungs for a minute or so enlivens the cells and prepares you for the exercise.

Close your eyes and sink into whatever surface you are resting on. Just flop into it and feel secure.

You are going to take your mind gently back to the time when you were one year old. You are unlikely to remember this but you may have seen a photograph of yourself then. If so, recall this and try to enter the mind of the baby that was you. If you have no photograph or memory of one, know that at this time you had probably begun to take solid food and begun to say your first words, maybe even short phrases.

If you still find this difficult to imagine, take yourself forward to your first childhood memories, see these as vividly as you can and then take your mind backwards. For example, if you can remember age three, see that and then go back to age two, trying to pull up whatever information you can. Then go back to age one.

Allow yourself a few moments to imagine this so that your memory cells can begin to give you a bit more information. Don't worry if you still can't seem to remember anything. Your brain certainly does have some recollection but you may only sense it as a vague feeling. The one important thing is that you are attempting to reach this memory.

Now, very gently, take yourself back across the preceding twelve months. Count them very slowly down: eleven . . . ten . . . nine . . . eight . . . seven . . . six . . . At each count try to imagine yourself back at this age: five . . . four . . . three . . . two . . . one.

Now count back the days of this first month of your life. We will begin at thirty: twenty-nine . . . twenty-eight . . . Imagine yourself as you were then. Keep counting back all the way to one and see yourself back safe and sound in your mother's womb. You are comfortable and secure here. What are your feelings? Do you have any thoughts? Any ideas about the life that is to come?

The chances are that all you will know is security and trust. Imagine how different your life would be if you had managed to retain this essential foundation.

Now you may know from your mother what sort of birth you had but in this exercise you are going to forget it and reinvent a new birth for yourself – a birth that was easy, harmonious, without pain or trauma. You slide into the world and the umbilicus is not cut right away. Cutting the umbilicus immediately after birth is a Western procedure, when in fact the umbilicus is designed to go on working until the lungs open naturally to breathe rather than gasping as a result of shock. You are making an easy adjustment to your new environment, still feeling secure and full of trust.

Now in this trustful, secure state, what do you feel you want to do with the life ahead? Is there some image that comes to mind? Or a vague feeling?

With hindsight you know that you have the personalities and lives of your parents to deal with and the environment into which you were born. So bypass now any difficulties you may have had and reinvent the ideal environment for yourself. See it in as much detail as you can and retain that sense of security and trust.

Take yourself forward to the age of three or four and see the kinds of game you were playing. What would you love to be doing? Is this ideal environment very different from the one your wrote down in your blueprint? Or is it fairly similar?

Now gently take yourself through a reinvented childhood. See the kinds of game you would play, the friends you would have, the kind of school you would have gone to. You may have been perfectly happy with your actual childhood; if so, simply add a few details.

If not, now is your chance to recreate it and put into it the things or kinds of people you would have liked.

See it all in as much detail as you can and take yourself up to the age of 12 or 13.

What are your hopes and dreams for the future now? In this relaxed state, set yourself goals for your reinvented life and know that you have begun to open channels in your mind that will make adjustments for you.

Take as much time as you like for this and then, when you are ready, take a few long deep breaths. Move your body a little. Maybe have a good stretch before you open your eyes.

You now need to get your blueprint from Chapter 2 and add any new information or details that have emerged from this exercise.

Compare this with your earlier statements for three years of age and adolescence.

Now that you are back to your everyday awareness, do any of your ideas or plans from this exercise seem odd or impossible?

Compare your blueprint with the results of this exercise very carefully and see what adjustments you might like to make to your lists. Do you want to amalgamate them? Or do you want to jettison some things from your earlier blueprint and incorporate new ones from this exercise? You have done a lot of work on your blueprints and it is time now to write out a neat, new list from the insights you have received, putting the most important things at the top.

A lot of people only get feelings rather than specific

images and if this is the case for you, simply write the feelings down. You have made contact with a fundamental aspect and expectation for yourself and if it is not part of your life now, your own subconscious will begin to use it and develop it now that you have opened a channel. It is literally part of your psyche that is waiting to be born.

Alex's Story

Alex was a high-flying businessman with a degree from Cambridge, a large house, a wife, two children, two BMWs and a villa in Spain. The lifestyle of his family was enviable but Alex wasn't happy and his blood pressure was high. His doctor had told him to slow down and had put him on medication for the blood pressure.

When I first saw him he appeared relaxed and blasé about his situation but his hands were covered with worry lines (see Chapter 9). His marriage line (Chapter 7) was fragmented and the mounts of Moon on both hands were fleshy and full. This indicated a deeply intuitive man whose success had been based both on his ability to handle people and on his sixth sense in knowing which deals to go for and which to leave alone.

When he did this exercise his reinvented life had nothing to do with manufacturing business at all. His images were of a quiet life close to the land or sea free from worry and pressure.

He promised he would take some action on this, but didn't. Eighteen months later his wife left him and he suffered a stroke. He was only 37.

He had no choice but to take sick leave, and during those convalescing months he decided to sell his huge manor house and Spanish villa and bought a cottage (not a small one – Alex's image of his environment was of space and size) with a large garden instead. His company offered him a much less stressful position that was less well paid.

Alex discovered that his finances are actually improving

now that he is more relaxed and has the time to do the things that are important to him. Unfortunately, the change did not bring his wife back but he does now have a permanent girlfriend.

During this exercise many people have an image of their lifespan as one of bliss and realise that fear and anger had entered almost at the moment of birth – fear for survival and anger at the disruption to their peaceful pre-birth world. Since most of us start life like this it is hardly surprising that we tend to be defensive and often sabotage ourselves.

The next exercise is to help to bring you back into alignment with your intuition and begin to trust yourself more.

Uncovering the Routines Which Run Your Life

This needs to be done when you have a free day or morning. You need to be left alone or at least without pressure from family or friends. The purpose is to free you from your reasoning, fearful self and it is a good idea to have a pen and paper handy to jot down any insights you may have.

The night before

Don't read a newspaper, watch the news on TV or a violent film two hours before you go to bed. Do everything you can to relax. Have a milk drink if you like, and a soak in a warm bath for half an hour or so. Listen to soothing music and, rather than read anything that will put other people's ideas into your head, take a pen and paper and write something yourself. This can be about your day, your life or simply jot down the first idea that comes into your head and develop it into a stream of consciousness or story.

When you get to bed and switch off the light, tell yourself that you are going to have a nourishing night's sleep and that you will receive any information you need when you wake up.

Step 1

When you wake up, can you remember any dreams? If so, jot them down.

Step 2

Lie straight back down again and *do nothing*. Don't do anything until you are prompted to, and make sure you know why you are doing it.

The obvious thing is that you're going to need the loo. So when you do, go, and come straight back to bed again.

At some point you are probably going to feel a desperate urge to get up. Examine your feelings. If it is because you're hungry or thirsty, that is physical, so go and get your drink or whatever and come back to bed.

Now just lie there. How do you feel? Lazy? Desperate to do something? If you feel tired, examine the causes of this. Is it overwork? Is it because certain problems are draining your energy? This is the time both to take a short rest and to take a good look at your life.

If you are feeling uncomfortable about lying there, what thoughts are prompting you? Do you feel edgy and not quite right about staying in bed? If so, who says so? Who gave you this idea? Have you had this idea all your life? Do you feel comfortable with it? If not, it is time to change it.

Make a note of your thoughts. For example, they might be:

- I always get up at eight.

- Only lazy people stay in bed all day.

- The devil makes work for idle hands to do.

- It's a waste of a day to stay in bed.

These could be turned round to the following affirmations:

- I am free to get up when I want.

- I have some of my most creative ideas when I'm in bed.

- I don't believe in the devil so it can't affect me.

- It is my body and my life. I'm living to the full whether I'm in bed or not.

The purpose of this exercise is not to suggest that your life would be better spent lazing around in bed, but to reveal to you what thoughts are driving you. Many of us are guilt-ridden about not being seen to be busy. We feel we have to justify ourselves, especially if we live with other people. On the other hand, there are others who have no difficulty in lazing around at all.

By exploring these early morning drives many people begin to uncover a very different pace of life to the one they have been living. By living at your own pace you will automatically become happier and more successful – you switch on to your own autopilot.

Step 3

For the rest of the morning (or day if that's the amount of time you've given yourself), *you act on your first thought* as much as possible as long as it's legal and it's not going to harm someone else. You can jot down your second thoughts if you like to remind you what they were.

Your first thought is an intense part of your psyche wanting to be heard.

Your second thoughts are your reasoning mind.

If you have first thoughts like 'I'd love to go out on a spree and spend £1,000' and you actually only have £10 to your name, obviously it is better *not* to act on these thoughts and run up credit. Instead, it is clear that you need to work on prosperity. Decide specifically what sum of money you would like and when you would like it by.

Write this down as a goal and use the techniques described in Chapter 3.

If you have first thoughts like 'I'm going to ring up so-and-so and tell them what I think about them', or 'I'm going round to see so-and-so and punch them on the nose', you are obviously distressed about a situation and need to look at it in detail.

Similarly, if you meet someone during this exercise who arouses a strong response in you – anger, annoyance, pleasure, attraction – it is a good idea to see if there is anything you can learn from it. For any of these you might like to try some role-play.

For this, you place a pillow or cushion on a chair and talk to it as if it were the person who has upset you. If punching someone on the nose was your feeling, punch the pillow instead. Allow all your anger and aggression to surface. Get into your feelings and see if there is some area of your life that could be improved. Perhaps you need to be more assertive or perhaps you're not getting enough admiration or recognition. *Decide* to do something towards improving your life. There will be more about this in other chapters. For example, if you want to improve your love life, see Chapter 6; your sex life, see Chapter 8; your work, look at Chapter 5.

Any first thoughts you have that you don't feel you can act on are trying to tell you about the limits you have created for yourself. There may be excellent reasons for the limits, like having a family and not feeling that you can take off for three months, for example. But it is doing you no good and will have a knock-on effect on everyone else around you if you are unfulfilled. So, without upsetting the foundation of such valuable limits, begin to introduce change that will improve your life. Look at your blueprint. There's bound to be something there that you can do right now, or something close to it. Enrol for the course, buy the glamorous shirt, change your hairstyle, arrange the holiday. Write some affirmations, do some power building from Chapter 3 or exercises from Chapter 5. I first did this exercise several

years ago when my youngest child had just started school.
I didn't feel liberated at the prospect because I'd spent so
many years in child-rearing that a humdrum day had become
routine and ingrained. I was an institutionalised mum.

My first thought when I'd seen them off to school was,
'I'd just love to get in the car and drive and drive.
Anywhere.' My second thought was: 'You can't. What
if you're not back by 3.30?'

But my first thought persisted, so I rang a friend with
children the same age as mine and asked her to pick mine
up if I wasn't back.

And then I did it. I just drove and drove. I remember
it so well. It was a Monday. I clocked up 200 miles and
drove across two counties. I had a nice lunch in a strange
town and bought, of all things, a new umbrella. It wasn't
raining but the umbrella looked so cheerful. I also bought
myself some Chanel handcream, although I'd never bought
anything other than cheap stuff before.

Both of these were first thoughts, and the sense of
liberation they gave me together with the trip itself was
brilliant. It didn't matter that my friends said 'You bought
an umbrella! You give yourself *carte blanche* for the day
and that's the best you can do. You're even more boring
that we thought.'

The only thing that mattered was that for whatever
Freudian reasons, I was doing *exactly* what I wanted. It
let in the first chink of light and paved the way to a vastly
expanded life and prosperity.

The only proviso with this exercise is that you can't
really include other people. You can't take them with you
or it won't work: they will keep you from following your
thoughts through, unless, of course, you've taken them along
as a watchdog to make sure you don't do something that you
might regret.

Similarly, if you suddenly have a first thought like 'I
want to jump into bed with my lover', and they comply,
the exercise is going to end up more to do with relationship
than your other inner drives. While many of us would not

pass up the chance of a luxurious romp, this exercise is to uncover other basic drives. When I lived in Spain I knew several people who began by feeling that it was their life's work to eat, drink and make love. Five months was about the longest any of them lasted before boredom set in, but because sex is such an overwhelming drive it is a good idea to look beyond it to see what else is there.

Step 4

Review your morning or day. Did it move along like any other day or was it substantially different? Did you at any time have a second thought saying 'I can't do that'? If so, what did you do? Did you act on your first thoughts or did you follow your second? Look at any situations like this very carefully. What are you doing to yourself? Are you always denying yourself the things you really want to do? To go on like this will eventually dry you up. So begin to build those 'first thought' things into your life a little more.

If your first thoughts seem off the map to you, there is part of your personality that is being suppressed and you need to begin to create a framework for your life that can include it; thoughts like:

- I'd like to go to Heathrow and take the first plane to Hawaii.

- I'd like to lie on a luxurious bed and be made love to by someone gorgeous and adoring – or maybe even several someones.

- I'd like to stay at home and recreate my garden.

- I'd like pots and pots of money so I never have to think about working for it again.

I had several thoughts like that and the biggest surprise

to me was that I am actually rather lazy. None of my friends believed me because I'm conscientious and try to do what's expected of me. Not any more. To be lazy and allow my thoughts to drift gives me pleasure and I needed more money to be able to fulfil this, so I set about creating it. It was relatively easy. If I can, you can too. Money is the easiest thing to create. It responds to thought faster than almost anything else. You don't have to agonise over it or do anything illegal to attract it. All you basically have to do is to decide how much you want and how you intend to live when you've got it and begin to make it real to your mind. All of the exercises in this book will help you to achieve this.

Reinvent Your Attitude

This exercise will seem to be the opposite of the previous one, but in fact the effect is often similar: it begins to release you from your habitual thinking.

Step 1

Give yourself an amount of time, say between an hour and a whole morning, but not a day when you're working.

During this time you try not to exercise your will. You remain passive. You are going to drift on events. There may be certain routines to your day, such as getting up, having a shower, having breakfast. Go through all these routines, paying close attention to the actual performance of them. Don't judge them. Don't *think* about them. If a thought arises, just be aware of it as if you are an observer and then let it go.

If it is a Saturday morning, for example, you may find yourself at a loose end after the initial routines. Your active mind will be urging you forward. Be aware of it but try not to act on it.

If you have family or friends with you, go along with

anything they suggest. Again don't judge anything, just pay attention to them and everything you do. Don't judge *them* either. Just be passive but pay attention.

If you are completely on your own and you come to the end of your routines, you can act on a first thought as in the previous exercise but allow the action to occupy your attention until it has been completed. Don't let other thoughts come and jostle you to act on them.

For example, you may suddenly think 'I'll go and clean out my wardrobe', and just a short while into doing it, another thought comes: 'This is boring, I think I'll go down to the pub.' Ignore this and stick with clearing out the wardrobe, paying attention to the movement of your body, the colours and sensation of your clothes, the empty space that is appearing and the thought process as you decide what to keep and what to throw out.

What happens for most people is that life impinges. The telephone rings and sets in train a whole new set of possibilities. You decide to pull a few weeds in the garden and a neighbour stops for a chat. Allow yourself to flow along with anything that comes up like this, and pay close attention to your feelings, to actually being where you are.

The idea here is to switch off the active, planning left brain (controlling your right hand) to uncover the creative right brain (controlling your left hand). This is good, passive Moon activity.

Many people are surprised at how much they take for granted and become aware of how much they have allowed themselves to be swept along by circumstances and other people. They also often see their friends and family in a new light and it can be very invigorating and releasing. Many people rediscover love and affection that has been buried by routine. Some people, by contrast, realise that some relationships have been outgrown.

Together, these two exercises (uncovering routines and reinventing your attitude) give you the experience of some of your driving forces and some of the things that you have either consciously suppressed or have allowed to be swamped by routine. This is your life and this is how you are living it. Life is precious, and you can change it right now.

As soon as you have completed both exercises, re-evaluate your life. If you are frustrated in any area, consider what you could do right now to introduce change. Check your blueprint:

(a) see if there is anything you want to add to it as a result of the exercises; and

(b) choose something from it right now so that you can begin to do what you really want with your minutes, hours and days.

Malcolm's Story

Malcolm was rather like Alex: he had a high-powered job in London and spent several months of the year travelling all over the world. He was the boyfriend of Mandy who was doing these exercises and, after some persuasion by her, joined her in them.

He was amazed to discover how much he had grown to hate the pressure and wanted to enjoy the kind of living that these exercises revealed to him.

He found the exercise in Chapter 8, 'Uncovering Your Own Dynamic Energy', on page 148 especially helpful. He realised that he had spent his entire life trying to seek approval and doing things to please others rather than himself. This applied to both his work and his family: he had trapped himself in a high-powered lifestyle that was never his own real choice.

Starting slowly, he began to work out strategies for the life he wanted, setting goals by deciding how much money he needed, where he wanted to live and what kind of work he wanted to do. He used, amongst other things, the magnetising and power-building exercises in Chapter 3 to get these off the ground.

He now lives in Hampshire, running his own consultancy from home where he can plan his work and free time to suit himself.

It took Malcolm several months before he realised that he could become self-employed. But it was two years before he made the move to Hampshire. During those interim years he built up contacts, and during the last six months he began trial runs for his new business. As a result, the final transition into his 'reinvented' life was smooth.

Starting a Dream Diary

Keeping a dream diary does not have to become a chore. If you get yourself a notebook to keep by the bed, on those mornings when you do remember your dreams you can quickly jot them down. After a while, when you reread them you may see a pattern emerging. You may have a few recurrent themes such as often appearing with friends or people that upset you. These will often be accompanied by a feeling throughout the day, so you should note this down as well. Is it a happy feeling or does it depress you? If the latter, you probably know why and may need to build up your self-esteem. Many of the exercises in this book will help you with this.

Most of us have the experience at some time or other of desperately trying to escape from terror and just being rooted to the spot. This is an anxiety dream and means that you may need to work on relationships or work. I used to have these until about six years ago when I suddenly found that I could fly in my dreams. Along would come the bogeyman and I would just lift off, high in the sky way out of reach. At this time I had begun working on the techniques in this book and in my other book, *Take Control of Your Life*.

You will know when you have major dreams. You know

the ones where the flavour of the dream stays with you all day. If it is a nightmare you will quickly work out what the problem is and can work on it. If it is a happy dream of love and fulfilment, healing at some level will have taken place. Check over the previous few days to see if you can discover a trigger for this dream. If you can, try to introduce more such occurrences into your life.

For example, Julie had a good job in a development laboratory in industry but was finding it difficult to deal with her mainly male colleagues. She had a lot of anxiety dreams until one night she dreamt of being loved and protected by some strange man.

She woke up feeling relaxed and good about herself. She discovered that her trigger had been to give a lift home to one of her colleagues whose own car had broken down and realising that he was human and not out to get her. On further examination, Julie became aware that she had a problem around men in general and her own love and sex life was arid. She did a lot of the exercises in this book and began to lighten up.

She is bright and was promoted at work, but still finds it difficult to strike the right balance with men at work. Personally, however, she now has a boyfriend and is coming to terms with both her own womanliness and the fact that she has to give men orders at work.

Tone Your Body

The Moon energy has an effect on the water in our body, especially the flow of lymph which transports toxins and waste matter from the cells. If we become emotionally or physically clogged or sluggish the lymph can become stuck in the nodes and leave us feeling and looking unwell. People with well-developed mounts of Moon tend to be more susceptible to this.

In order to move the lymph in the body, muscle action from exercise is effective. Any form of aerobic exercise, including walking and swimming, is good. But for clearing the pelvic lymph nodes some of the best are yoga ones.

Clearing pelvic lymph

Step 1
Sit on the floor, back straight with legs stretched as far apart as possible without undue strain. Place your hands on the floor in front of you and slowly 'walk' them forward until you feel slight tension at the top of your thighs. Hold for a few seconds and then release. You can repeat it once or twice. At first you may not be able to move more than an inch or two but this increases quite quickly with practice.

Step 2
Still sitting on the floor, legs out straight, bend your knees and bring the soles of your feet together until they are touching. Gently move your knees towards the floor until you feel tension. At first the angle of your legs from the floor could be as much as 90 degrees if you are very stiff.

Rest your hands on your knees and gently rock them up and down. The pose is called the butterfly, which will give you some idea of the motion you are aiming for: your bent legs should move up and down like butterfly wings.

Both these exercises are excellent for toning up the genitals as well, so if you're feeling under par sexually, these should give you a boost.

Face

The lymph in the face often gets very little stimulus to move. These simple exercises will not only clear it and make you feel better; they are also excellent for brightening and lifting the skin.

When you have five minutes or so, sit down and take the three middle fingers of each hand and place them horizontally on the forehead above the bridge of the nose. Press gently and then move them slowly across the forehead, pressing as you go, so that the whole forehead has been contacted.

Now turn the fingers vertically, placing them on the cheekbone below your eyes. Press again in the same way, moving outwards towards your ears.

Return your fingers to the cheekbone but place them just below the last position and press gently. Move your fingers in a gently pressing movement out towards your ears.

Repeat this process several times, moving your fingers a little lower each time until you reach your jawbone.

This time, take the thumb and forefinger of each hand, placing the thumbs beneath the jawbone and forefingers on the upper side so that you have the jawbone pinched between them. Press gently and pinch all along the jaw to your ears. A lot of tension is held here, so you may like to repeat it several times.

Finally, place both forefingers on the bone behind the ear and press gently in a circular motion, moving the skin over the bone. If there are any painful spots, work over these a bit more.

You can also take thumb and forefinger and pinch gently over your earlobes and along the edge of the ear. It is believed that the ear corresponds to our 'foetal' selves, the lobe representing the head, the curve of the ear the spine; and massaging it in this way can contact old imbalances in the system and help to heal them.

Charging up your water energy

Whether your mount of Moon is full or flattened, physically making contact with water will help to balance it.

A daily shower helps to cleanse the electromagnetic field around our bodies. This can become quite depleted and contaminated if we have been under stress or exposed to negative emotions in ourselves or others. This may sound simple – most of us do it anyway – but it isn't just being cleaner that makes us feel better after a shower. It is this subtle cleansing too.

Try turning the shower to *cold* for a few seconds and then back to warm, but warn anyone living with you first! The gasping you're likely to make will sound as if you're either ill or having an orgasm.

If you do this several times, it will assist the passage of lymph, help your hair and nails to grow, tone the skin, and, surprisingly, help to lower your blood pressure.

The same is true of baths. If you do have high blood pressure, the following method is much less shocking to the system.

Don't have your bath too hot but soak in it as long as you feel comfortable. Before you get out, release the plug and let some water go. Replace the plug and refill from the cold tap while you are lying there. Do this several times until the water is cool or cold, and then get out.

This is a superb stimulant to the system. It enhances the function of the kidneys, thereby releasing water locked in the tissues along with excess toxins.

Swimming has the same effect plus the added bonus of the exercise. But best of all is the sea, where you have the massaging action of the waves and the detoxifying effect of the minerals and salt.

By using any of these techniques you will begin to open up more to your intuition. You will begin to *feel* what you want to do with your life rather than organising it with your mind. The more you allow your intuition to inform your actions, the more you will discover that the mount of Moon on your hands is filling out and becoming more rounded in appearance. Your intuition is never wrong and will guide you into a richer and more fulfilling life.

5

Career and Lifestyle: Jupiter

If one advances confidently in the direction of their dreams and endeavours to lead a life which they have imagined, they will meet with a success unexpected in common hours.

(Thoreau)

The attributes of Jupiter are not so well known as those of the Sun and Moon, but anyone interested in astrology will know that it rules the zodiac sign of Sagittarius, the Archer. As such it is associated with travel, expansion and a warm, fun-loving personality. Jupiter is also connected with our need to expand and develop our lives, not just in work and career, but in any direction that makes us feel that progress is being made. This can encompass friendships, travel, study, hobbies, openness to new ideas and, indeed, anything that *moves* us forward.

Jupiter is also associated with bonhomie, conviviality, good times and from the Latin root comes the word 'joviality'. Following on from this, the Jupiter energy is also linked with weight gain, the middle-age spread.

Now, you will quite naturally be wondering how this applies to you. Your hands will give you the answer.

Astrology is a complicated science but the study of your own hands makes understanding yourself easy. Most people know their own sun sign – the position of the sun when you were born, making you a Libra or a Gemini, an Aries and so on. But this will not help you to understand the powerful interactions of all the planets. For example, although Jupiter is the planet which rules Sagittarius, I have encountered few Sagittarians who have the Jupiter 'weight' difficulty. This comes when the planet Jupiter is in a difficult position in relation to other planets, and a glance at your own hands will show what all this means to you.

The finger of Jupiter is the index finger, as shown in Figure 5.1.

The ideal configuration is for the Jupiter finger to be full and the phalanges well balanced, in size and length, with each other. It is also a good sign if the fingers of Jupiter and the Sun (third finger) are of a similar length.

If the finger of Jupiter is longer than Sun, as in Figure 5.2, it means that you have Jupiter strongly aspected in your horoscope, that you are a go-getter by nature no matter what your circumstances, that you hate life to be static. You will work hard to get what you want and, provided that the finger of Sun is full and well balanced despite its shorter length, you will probably succeed. Check your hands for Sun lines too (see Chapter 3), which will show you when your efforts are likely to succeed.

Don't worry if your finger of Jupiter is full and long and there is an absence of Sun lines, or the finger of Sun is wasp-waisted on any of the phalanges. The exercises in this chapter and under 'Sun' will help to balance things up and will bring success and fulfilment into your life faster.

If the finger of Jupiter is shorter than the finger of Sun, as in Figure 5.3, it means that you have more of a problem with Jupiter. The strong finger of Sun can indicate a devil-may-care attitude (see Chapter 3) but the short Jupiter indicates that you tend to let other people's needs get in the way of your own. You can easily be discouraged or diverted from your goals and convince yourself that the life you opt for is the right one.

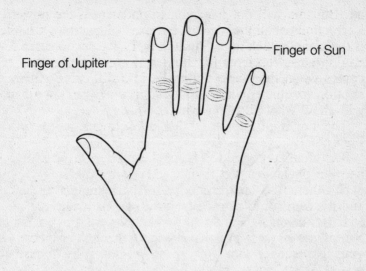

Figure 5.1

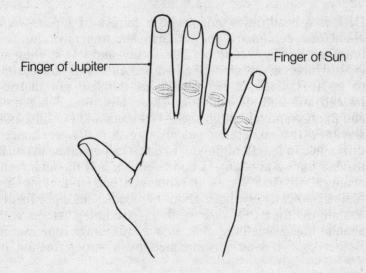

Figure 5.2

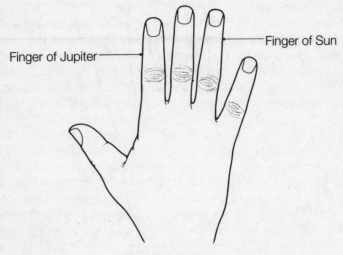

Finger of Jupiter

Finger of Sun

Figure 5.3

Beth's Story

Beth is a beautiful woman whose fingers of Jupiter were about one centimetre shorter than her fingers of Sun on both hands. She was in her late forties and just starting an Open University course. She had had a 'sort of half-desire' to go to college in her late teens but had got married instead and had six children. These took up all her time and energy and, although she loved them and her husband, she knew that something was missing. A really pronounced difference in length of fingers like this can continue to cause trouble until something is done about it and the alignment changes. In Beth's case it sabotaged her by making her feel periodically apathetic about her studies until she finally abandoned them. Of course, there is nothing wrong with abandoning something that is not fulfilling you, but in Beth's case it was accompanied by a strong feeling of losing the whole point of life. She just didn't know what to do with herself.

The techniques which follow helped to get her back on track, but before we go on to these I will mention the other interesting problem that some of you may discover: the discrepancy between right and left hands. In Beth's case the Jupiter finger was shorter on *both* hands but in some cases it is *long* on one hand and *short* on the other, as in Figure 5.4.

You will remember that the left hand represents our innate and inner subconscious selves whereas the right hand represents our outgoing and active, conscious selves; so if your finger of Jupiter is longer on the left hand than on the right it means that inwardly you are deeply ambitious and longing to achieve progress in your life. The shorter Jupiter on your right hand means that, for some reason, you have been thwarted. This could be of your own making; you may have allowed the desires of others to hold you back. This often relates to family. Parents usually have strong

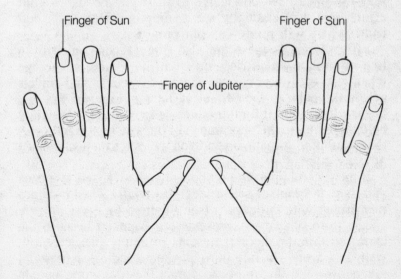

Figure 5.4

blueprints for their own lives and hopes for their children which can create havoc if a child is of a very different temperament. In older people I have seen this work in two ways, especially with women.

Many women born before the Second World War grew up with the idea that marriage and family was a job in itself; anyone wanting to forge ahead was regarded as something of an anomaly and the opportunities were simply not there as they are today. Similarly, their parents expected to be cared for in old age and yet, as these women grew older, they saw the next generation enjoying more freedom than they had ever had. Those that have either a longer left finger of Jupiter or short Jupiters on both hands feel that they have missed out or tend to regard the world as heading for disaster because the structures with which they grew up have been eroded.

If you have a long finger of Jupiter on the right hand but not on the left it means that you have made a conscious effort to achieve progress although your early circumstances may not have been conducive to it. If you persist in your efforts you will gradually see an improvement in the left hand, which will reinforce your progress.

Efforts such as these are also often accompanied by a line of Jupiter which rises up from the lifeline at the age when you are initiating the course of action, and travels across the palm to the Mount of Jupiter (Figure 5.5).

New lines appear on our hands as a result of persistently held thoughts, so the appearance of lines of Jupiter indicates that your mind is made up and you have an excellent chance of success.

If the second phalange is short or wasp-waisted, it means that there is a lack of self-esteem, especially when it comes to working with colleagues (see Figure 5.6).

The third phalange represents our connectedness to the earth, so thinness here represents difficulty in successful, well-paid work. A full third phalange indicates personal magnetism and the ability to attract the life, work, people and money you want.

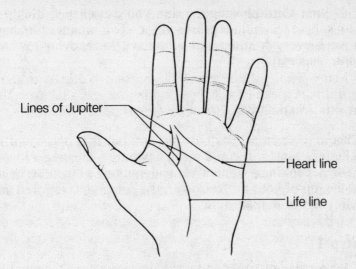

Figure 5.5

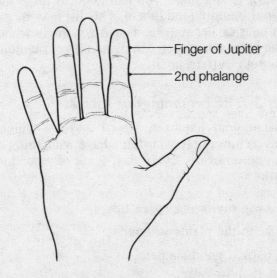

Figure 5.6

If your third phalange is thin you can change it. Just a few simple techniques practised for a few minutes for about a week every so often will soon have you moving towards more success.

What is Success for You?

This may seem an obvious question but it is one we often take for granted. It could mean anything – creating a lovely garden, cooking a wonderful meal, running a business, being at the top of your profession or just doing your job well and enjoying your spare time.

Step 1

Take a piece of paper and write down what makes you feel successful. Include the apparently small things, like some task well done, as well as a larger ambition which either has made or would make you feel good. If these things are not on your blueprint, add them. This list may be more specific than your earlier statements and you are now moving closer to the point where you can blend all your childhood dreams with your current goals.

Step 2: The beginnings of success

Look at your list from Step 1 and see which things are easily achieved. If you don't have something on your list that you do nearly every day, think of something now, for example:

- keep my living space tidy,
- keep the plants watered,
- cook a good supper.

It is important that each day is filled with small successes so that you begin to see the continuity between these and larger ones.

Now look at the things on your list that seem harder and that you may have some doubt about.

Step 3: Make affirmations

Use these to link the easy and difficult things together. For example:

1. Every time I cook my supper I am one step nearer to making £X,000.

2. Every time I water the plants I am also nourishing my ability to get the job I want.

3. Every time I hoover the carpet/wash up I am also clearing the path towards my successful promotion.

4. Every time I cook a wonderful meal I am enhancing my ability to learn that new language.

Please note, however, that if you have days when you don't enjoy your supper or have left your room a tip you do not say 'Everything's a mess and I feel terrible. I'll never get anywhere.' Forgive yourself, forget any lapses and affirm that you are progressing anyway.

All this may seem a bit bizarre at first, but what you are doing is similar to the power building described in Chapter 3. You are giving your mind and body the experience of success with something tangible and implanting the suggestion of success with something that is more out of reach.

The mind readily accepts new concepts like this. Think of the number of times you have given it negative suggestions: 'Oh, I'll never manage that.' 'So-and-so's much better than me, I may as well give up.' 'Damn, I've burnt the toast. I can't even get a simple thing like that right.'

Yes, I know. Often. So now you're going to change it and create a success consciousness for yourself to speed you towards the life you really want.

Accessing the Larger Ambitions for Our Lives

You know what your early ambitions are from your blue-print, but have they changed? Circumstances can often uncover latent abilities that we never knew were there. Quite often we find ourselves trapped in a wage-earning situation to finance lifestyle or family and our frustration can often lead to new ambitions for ourselves. As a result, many of the apparent difficulties of our culture – such as unemployment, and the advance of technology, which creates new careers as fast as it makes others redundant – should actually be seen as an opportunity for us to expand ourselves.

Visualisation

You may find it helpful to tape this exercise or get someone to read it to you. Find a time when you will be uninterrupted for ten or fifteen minutes, sit down and close your eyes. Relax as much as you can by tensing your muscles and then releasing them. Breathe deeply a few times into your abdomen, relaxing a little more at each breath.

Take your mind back to the time when you were between 16 and 22. If you are in this age group, just look at your life now. This is a time of major life choices for most people.

Now take your awareness away from your brain down to the area of your heart. You may find it helpful to imagine your awareness as a ball of light that is spiralling slowly downwards from your head to your heart. It doesn't matter if you can't visualise this; your intention will create the result that is right for you.

In this relaxed state ask your heart what you really want

to do. What is the work that you would love to be doing? What is the lifestyle that you would love to be having? You can project this a few years forwards as well if you like, so that you get a more complete picture. Put in as much detail as you can imagine and make it as real as possible with colours, sounds and scents. Again if you don't see well in pictures it doesn't matter: whatever way you think with your imagination will create results.

Now gently allow your awareness to rise back to your head or allow the ball of light to spiral upwards, if that is the image you have used. Here in your head is where logic and reason reside.

Now what negative ideas have logic and reason put there? What ideas have other people put there? Has anyone told you that you can't fulfil a particular ambition? Has anyone said that it is too difficult, too expensive? Consider these ideas for a moment and then take them back down to your heart with your awareness as a ball of light and ask your heart what it has to say about them.

Your heart never lies. It will tell you what you need to know.

Repeat this process for any age when you had to make a life-changing decision. Allow the decision and the reasoning behind it to fill your head for a few moments, then take your awareness down to your heart and ask if there is anything that could have been done better or differently, if there are any other factors that should have been taken into consideration.

Finally, and most importantly, bring your awareness to the qualities of your life right now. Using the image of the ball of light if it appeals to you, go into your heart and ask what directions you should be seeking now. What lifestyle or change in career is the best move for you now? Allow your heart to give you as much information as possible. This will come in the form of feelings and possibly images. If you seem to get nothing, it is temporary. Any intention you have will be accepted by your heart and you will have the answers within a few hours, or at most a day or two.

Now take your awareness as a ball of light downwards into your gut area, the area of intuition. Take all the feelings and information from your heart with you and ask your intuition to tell you how to apply this in your life. You may get an answer right away, but it doesn't matter if you don't. The intuition will merge all the information and present it to your brain within a few hours or a day or two in the form of *knowing* that a course of action is right.

You can help to speed the process by allowing the light-ball of awareness to spiral gently up through your body to your heart and then spiral up again to your brain. Relax for a few moments and when you are ready, open your eyes.

On a piece of paper jot down briefly any ideas, insights or information that you received. This gives your brain and ego the comfort of knowing that it hasn't been bypassed and that it can check out any ideas. The real blending will be done by all three areas – brain, heart, intuition – but the brain is so used to being in charge it needs a bit of encouragement to accept new ways of doing things.

When the first promptings come they may be quite simple things but accompanied by a strong feeling of well-being and rightness. But if you are ready for a major change – and if the groundwork has already been laid by you, you will have a Sun line or Jupiter line rising up from the line of life – you may get an overwhelming propulsion towards a particular course of action.

Ten years is represented on the lifeline by approximately one centimetre; so if you have a line of Sun touching your lifeline at approximately 3.5 centimetres, you are due for change at around the age of 35. This will be change that you have already created by your previous thoughts.

But remember – this book is all about creating the change that you want; so if you have no beneficial lines ahead of you on your lifeline and you want them, these exercises all begin the alteration of the mental processes which create the lines on your hands. The more you use these techniques the faster the lines will alter and beneficial change will occur in your life.

Although success always comes from the practice of these exercises, some of the answers obtained from doing the above exercise can be surprising.

Judy's Story

Judy was bright and had wanted to go to university when she left school. Her parents were very old-fashioned and believed that a woman's place was in the home. They actively discouraged her, and when she was in her early twenties she married a university lecturer. She knew in her heart then that she was doing it partly to get close to her thwarted dream, and did in fact get accepted as an undergraduate and succeeded in obtaining a good degree. Her husband was a mirror of her parents and had wanted a wife who would look after him. He hated her preoccupation with her studies and the marriage got into such difficulties that Judy left him. They had no children so she blithely thought that she was simply leaving a bad affair.

She began a brilliantly successful career in commerce and for several years developed it until she was a director of a company making medical supplies, and had an excellent salary, perks and travel. But she was unfulfilled emotionally. She wanted a close, loving relationship, but each man she met was either married, or divorced with children and payments to an ex-wife, or a confirmed bachelor. It seemed to her that she had everything to offer: no strings from another relationship, excellent finances and lifestyle – while the men she met were offering nothing.

She did the above exercise several times and whenever she moved her awareness to her heart she felt an unpleasant tightness. At one point she even thought she might have heart trouble. However, when she asked where the tightness came from she was immediately given the image of her husband and was filled with such rage that her whole body tensed up. She never remembered feeling rage against him. She had suppressed it while she furthered her career. Now she could see that her life had become unbalanced because she had not taken it into account.

By doing this exercise several times Judy began to get a balanced view of her former marriage, seeing that she was as much at fault as her husband, by not openly recognising that she had to a certain extent used him.

Judy's predicament had an unusual outcome. She decided to track down her husband, with whom she had lost contact. By this time he had left his university teaching post and was working in the United States for a computer company. He was even more successful than Judy, but had not remarried either, feeling as essentially lonely and emotionally unfulfilled.

They decided to have another attempt with their marriage and it has worked. Her husband recognised that he would never have an earth mother housekeeper in Judy and found it hard at first to accept the challenge of her success. He has also had to accept that she doesn't want children, but they have so much in common that they are now developing in ways that would not have been possible with other partners.

Building Success

We all need it. It is the very motivation of our existence and, at rock bottom, it is self-esteem, feeling good about our lives and the day well lived.

But we often sabotage ourselves with feelings of inadequacy or apathy which stop us feeling happy and can immobilise us. The following exercises are to uncover some of these feelings and help you to achieve your ambitions, large and small.

Step 1

Give your mind the experience of doing things differently. Go a different way to work or to the shops. If you normally

go by car, try going by bus. If you normally go by bus or
tube, try getting off a stop early and walking the rest of
the way.

Do your shopping in a different supermarket or store. Buy
different foods. Experiment with different types of cooking
– vegetarian, Chinese, Italian. Get out a recipe book, close
your eyes, flick over the pages and stop somewhere. Stick
a pin in the page. Open your eyes and decide to make the
dish your pin has indicated. Create a bit of adventure, a bit
of chance.

Step 2

Make a list of things you've never done before but would
like to. You could put them under the following headings:

a. things you might like to do;

b. things that fill you with fear;

c. places in England you've never been;

d. places in Europe you've never been;

e. places in the USA you've never been;

f. places in the world you've never been.

Now make a grid using the headings *easy*, *hard*, *expensive*
and *scary* and fill it out with your list.

Rachel's list looked like this.

Easy

- Take horseriding lessons
- Visit Denmark
- Have lunch at Le Manoir de Quatre Saisons
- Stay the night at a five-star hotel
- Watch polo

- Give up work
- Learn to ski

Hard

- Have my head shaved
- Ride in a point-to-point
- Spend a year in a New Age community

Expensive

- Fly in Concorde to the USA
- Visit Australia
- Visit Far East
- Own a Porsche
- Buy a designer outfit

Scary

- Hang Gliding
- Parachuting
- Rock Climbing
- Skiing off piste

No, I'm not going to suggest that you do something from each section. The largest section in Rachel's list is the 'easy' one, but it is also pretty expensive so she began to work on money in order to bring some expansion into her life.

If your 'scary' list is very long it would be a good idea for you to examine your fears. Are they of physical things like rock climbing or scuba diving? Social things like giving a speech or going alone to a party? Affirmations to work on your negative feelings will help.

Good sample affirmations would be:

I————am perfectly capable of being a good (rider/ski-er/swimmer)

I————now release my fears of (riding/skiing/swimming)

My fears come from my imagination, so I————now allow my imagination to create success in (riding/skiing/swimming)

Once you have contacted your root anxiety and affirm that you are now overcoming it, try to dilute something from your 'scary' list and do it. For example, if rock climbing is on your list, try hill walking instead; if you've put skiing off piste – not generally recommended anyway – try doing harder runs than usual.

Chris hated the water and couldn't swim so her list included things like swimming in deep water, diving off a rock into the sea. She diluted her list by taking swimming lessons, then increased her courage by going down the easy slide flumes at the pool first and advancing to the hardest 'black hole'.

She can now swim happily in deep water and knows that she doesn't need to dive off rocks into the sea unless she really wants to. Dealing with fear has a 'knock-on' effect in all other areas of our lives. It gives us more confidence.

Step 3: Making an imaginary film

If your 'scary' list contains some things that are less tangible, like 'going alone to a party' or 'meeting strangers', the following exercise will help you to deal with specific fears.

Sit down somewhere quiet and close your eyes. You are going to imagine that you are making a film of scenes from your life, that you are holding the camera.

Decide what you want to film. It can be something about which you are frightened or apprehensive; so see yourself in this picture as accomplishing everything with ease. See it in as much detail as possible just as if you were filming. Get the light right and the scenery or furniture. What are the clothes like, and the people wearing them? See yourself interacting with your environment and other people with ease, success and pleasure.

You can take this further if you like and allow your mind to make an imaginary film of the possibilities for your life, the kinds of thing your heart would love you to be doing.

Step 4

Put your list in a safe place and refer to it at least once a month. Try to do at least *one* thing, or one diluted thing, from it as soon as possible. Once you have managed this, check your list to see if it needs any adjustments and decide again to do one more thing as soon as possible.

Once you have managed two or three you will probably notice some significant overall improvements in your life.

Rachel's Story

You have already read Rachel's list (see p.81) and have probably formed a picture of her as some sort of extravagant airhead. In fact, she is aged 27 and was an infant teacher. She is very attractive, but by her own admission wears drab clothes and has led a rather mouselike existence. Her finger of Jupiter is long on her left hand but shorter on her right, and the second phalange of her Jupiter (index) finger on her right hand is thin, the joint overdeveloped, which is a sign of blocked energy.

Her father is a successful man but was away from home a great deal. Her mother is attractive but very screwed up about sex, which she regarded as rather dirty and only for child-bearing. She is also a pious churchwoman who gives her time to charity and church work. Rachel was a devoted churchwoman herself and at one time even considered becoming a nun. Her father talked her out of it and tried to arrange for her to go away to school for the sixth form to weaken her mother's influence. Her mother won. Rachel compromised and trained to be a teacher, seeing it as a way of helping others.

Although it was a good profession, she knew that she wanted something different but had no experience and was afraid. She felt guilty about her mother, whom she loved and didn't want to upset.

As you can see from Rachel's list, she has an adventurous spirit. She was encouraged to do something from her 'easy' list. She opted to go to an advanced language class and to take occasional riding lessons. She loved the riding and began to do it weekly, making new friends among the staff. There was a mobile home on site which had once served as an office. This was offered to Rachel free if she would check the horses before she went to bed every night.

It would have been a very difficult adjustment for her because her home was only a few miles away and it would have been obvious to her mother that she was trying to break away. She was frightened to confront her mother. Her mind seemed to go blank and she didn't know what she wanted.

This is a common problem when we've dug ourselves into a more or less comfortable rut; so Rachel went back to some of the exercises in Chapter 4, starting with exercise 2, Uncovering the Routines Which Run Your Life, (see p.53). She planned to lie in bed until prompted to move but her mother came in and started to nag her, telling her that her problem was all these newfangled ideas.

Rachel began to feel irritated and invaded. She tried to write some affirmations but her mother sensed that there was something going on and kept interrupting her. Rachel was at boiling point, realising that her mother was interfering because she felt threatened and that she would never let Rachel go unless Rachel forced the issue.

It shook her, so she decided to talk to her father. She couldn't even do this without her mother interfering, so she had to make an appointment to meet him at a pub for lunch. He gave her his blessing but didn't like the idea of her being in a mobile home except as a temporary measure. He gave her all the help he could and pacified her mother when Rachel decided to give up teaching. It had always been a compromise and she was feeling deeply frustrated. She did all the exercises in this chapter and 'seeing her life as film' revealed her as someone who was travelling and free.

As a result, she decided to try a job in a travel agent's. Her imagination was fired, so she moved to another travel company where she travels, trying out different resorts and hotels, and has a boyfriend. If she hadn't tried these exercises she might never have opened her mind to opportunity.

Dealing with Failure

This is an important aspect of the finger of Jupiter, especially if it is a bit on the weak side. We all come up against it at some time or other and some of the reasons for it are these:

1. aiming for something for which you are not properly equipped or qualified;

2. having a rigid attitude and expectation about results. For example, you might get a B when you wanted an A. To others you've succeeded but to you it might seem useless;

3. aiming for something for which you are properly qualified but the competition is too fierce;

4. being successful for a while but having it slip through your fingers as a result of circumstances 'beyond your control'.

The truth is that if there is something you want, you can have it – but not always in the exact way you expect. In other words you can have the *quality* of what you want.

For example, you might want to be Prime Minister and by the nature of the job it is only occasionally vacant. By aiming for it you may get there, but if you are realistic, you would be happy to end up in the Cabinet or as an MP. In the process of aiming for what they want, most people spend quite long periods in the doldrums before things start to shift; and in retrospect, most people realise that where they end up is really the perfect place for them to be. By aiming for what you think you want, your creative brain creates it in the way that is best for you.

Step 1

Sit down for a few minutes, close your eyes and recall your biggest failure, embarrassment or humiliation. Recall the setting and the people you were with. Now think very carefully about why this seemed so awful to you. Did it make you feel inadequate? If so, why? Did you feel that other people were superior to you? If so, in what way?

Are you sure that you're right about this? Look again. Is it really so important? Are the people who upset you really worth it? After all, they're only human. They've had their breakfast and been to the loo even if they like to appear too grand to have physical needs.

If it was an exam or interview you failed and it was a big ambition, don't give up. Decide whether it is still something you want and whether you have the right abilities. If so, follow these steps.

1. Write it down as a goal and write down when you want to achieve it by.

2. Write two or three affirmations around this goal ten times a day for one week every month for about three to six months, depending on how you're feeling.

3. Visualise yourself with this goal. Close your eyes and feel how it would be to have achieved it. See the life you will lead once it is achieved.

4. Look for results, no matter how small they may seem, as you move towards your goal. Be pleased about them. Be aware of new opportunities, new ways of doing things. Your creative mind will more than likely deliver your goal in a way that you don't expect.

I have to admit that getting my first book, *Take Control of Your Life*, published was like that. One of my ultimate ambitions had been to achieve success as a writer, but I had envisaged writing a novel and I saw myself being sufficiently well off to spend two or three months abroad every year writing my fiction. I also had this image of being interviewed on radio and TV and by papers and magazines about my books.

Well, I tried. My first novel received some very encouraging letters but no publisher actually accepted it. My second one was a complete disaster and received rude letters. By this time I was completely disheartened. I desperately wanted to break out of the professional rut I had dug for myself but couldn't see how.

I began to use the techniques in this book and in *Take Control of Your Life*, all the while affirming that I would make it as a writer. The first thing that happened was that my finances began to perk up in leaps and bounds. I began to feel wonderful about this and couldn't stop telling people about it. I used to meet friends for the 'prosperity lunches' described in the first book and decided that I would be, for a while, 'a lady who lunched'. During one of these lunches a friend asked me to send an outline of my ideas to a publisher. After much humming, hahing and 'is this what I really want?' I did. The publishers accepted it right away and here you are, reading my second book.

I am now perfectly happy with the way my writing ambitions have turned out, the more so because they may help you to become the success you want to be as well.

In fact, everything I had visualised around my writing goal happened. I simply hadn't visualised the writing of fiction strongly enough; so my mind presented me with the first writing opportunity. However, I do have enough money to take two or three months off if I want to; *BUT* – and this is a very important point – the money I needed came *before* the books.

Money is the easiest ambition to bring into reality; so if you feel stuck about your major ambitions, start working on smallish, specific amounts of money. You can include money in any of the visualisation techniques in the book – just pop an image of the amount and when you'd like it by at the end of any session. Do the same with affirmations, including the amount of money you would like and when you want it by.

At first most people don't achieve the total amount of money they've affirmed for but everyone creates some improvement. As your confidence grows you will find you succeed much more quickly.

What To Do If You Lose Your Job or Opt to Stay at Home with Children

This is becoming a choice many of us have to face: the possibility of being at home for an indefinite period. Whether you have been forced into it by loss of work or chosen it because of children, you can, of course, always look for other work as an employee. However, many of us fail to realise that we have unique abilities that can be uncovered and developed during a period at home. Instead of being a time of stagnation, it can become a time of growth.

Right now, at this very minute, you have skills and abilities that you can turn into cash.

Step 1

Make a list of all the things you can do, no matter how bizarre, whether it's cooking or mending fuses or becoming a whore or gigolo. There are literally hundreds of things you are capable of doing.

Step 2

Is there anything you would *like* to do on this list? If the answer is no, play around with some combinations of your list and see if you can come up with something new.

Step 3

Give yourself ten minutes every day to sit down, close your eyes and ask yourself, 'What could I do from home?' Do this every day until you get an answer. Make it a ritual at a specific time of day so you don't forget, say after coffee or tea. Many successful new businesses and enterprises have grown from apparent misfortune as a result of doing these simple exercises.

Finger of Jupiter and Deposit of Fats in the Body

As already mentioned, Jupiter is often associated with overweight and also with the function of the endocrine glands. Many causes of overweight are psychological and with reference to Jupiter it is often due to a feeling of being stuck. We all have Jupiter somewhere in our horoscope, and as it is the planet of expansion or movement, if we feel our lives are stagnating a few pounds can sometimes stagnate too. All the exercises in this chapter will help to unblock energy but you may find the following especially helpful.

- Break out of routine for a day or week. Go to different shops. Travel differently. Take the day off.

- Take a trip to a different town or to a different area.

- Eat different foods.

- Go to a different restaurant or pub.

- Take a break somewhere you've never been before.

- Do something you've never done before (as long as it's legal.)

- Go without a meal – breakfast, lunch or dinner – and see how you feel.

- When you wake up in the morning, decide what your most desired food is that day and make sure you eat it. How does it make you feel?

- Go to a supermarket when you have no weekly or family shopping to do and choose something delicious just for you. Eat it with pleasure and preferably alone. How do you feel?

- Go to a restaurant by yourself and choose something delicious just for you. Enjoy it.

Make a note of how any of these activities makes you feel and how it affects your body. Do you lose weight, gain weight, stay and feel the same? If these exercises bring improvement, decide to include them in your life more often.

We are bombarded daily with other people's ideas for our lives, so these exercises will help to bring your life back in line with its owner and liver – you.

Your body and mind are a complete unit: if you unblock the one you'll get a corresponding release in the other. Similarly, if you allow blocks in the one, the other will become blocked as well.

Overall, you don't need to do *all* the techniques in this chapter to create significant developments in your life. I would suggest that the visualisation on page 76 is essential to begin with, but incorporate any or all of the other exercises as your instinct tells you.

Whatever you feel like doing is always going to be the best thing for you. Never force yourself – it is usually some kind of force that sent you off track in the first place.

Remember that any exercise *you* are choosing to do is a gift to yourself, to get back in touch with your true self, and the patterns on your hands are a map of your journey.

6

Love Life and Desires: Venus

A long time I have loved the sunned mother-of-pearl
  of your body,
Until I even believe that you own the universe . . .
I want to have with you
What spring has with the cherry trees.

(Pablo Neruda)

The name Venus is associated in most minds with the
Goddess of Love, and although in relation both to astrology
and to the hand patterns it does have connections with love
and romance, it actually represents very much more.

The mount of Venus is situated at the base of the thumb
and spanned by the lifeline, as shown in Figure 6.1.

The fact that the lifeline is its outer perimeter reveals how
important it is. The lifeline reveals the length and quality
of our lives and represents our journey on this planet. The
mount of Venus beneath it is the bedrock of our lives, the
soil from which all our desires for our lives spring. If it is
full and fleshy it means that you have a passionate nature
and take on life wholeheartedly. If it is flatter, it means
that you are more reasoned in your approach.

Some people have a combination of these – full in one
section and flatter in another. If the fullness is near the
lifeline it means that you have a full-blooded approach to
life but that it is not fully supported by your ideas or feelings
about yourself. If the fullness is near the base of the thumb

and the mount is flatter near the lifeline, it means that you have a vigorous energy that is not being fully manifested in your life. In both these cases there is a block somewhere which can easily be changed.

Now, to get down to that all-important factor: love. The mount of Venus is where the affection lines arise on the palm. They cross the lifeline and for a good love relationship travel over the head and heart lines to the Mount of Mercury (see Figure 6.2). Each affection line you have represents a love bond of some sort. It is quite normal for single people to have quite a few of them stacking up; and I'm afraid I've seen quite a few married people with some that their spouses would be horrified about if they knew what they meant.

However, they don't all mean hot, passionate affairs. If they end at the head line (Figure 6.3) it means that the friendship or affection is not really leading anywhere emotionally but will probably have quite an impact on how you look at life. If they end at the heart line it means that

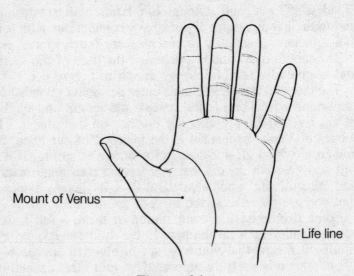

Figure 6.1

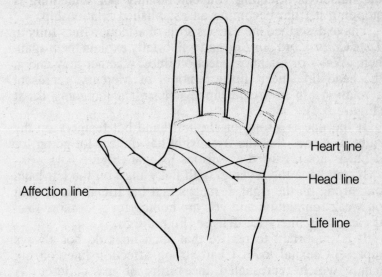

Figure 6.2

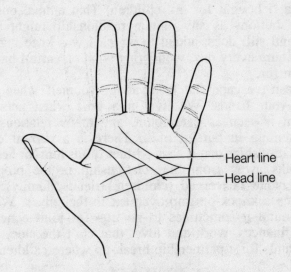

Figure 6.3

the liaison is affecting you emotionally but something is stopping it from becoming an established relationship.

I have described the various sorts of affection lines fully in *Take Control of Your Life* and will briefly explain them again here. Wavy or feathery affection lines, whether they end at the head line, heart line or mount of Mercury, represent a relationship or friendship that hasn't a lot going for it (Figure 6.4).

If the line is strong on the left hand but feathery on the right, it means that the friendship has quite a lot going for it but is not regarded as serious by you (Figure 6.4).

If you have the reverse, with flaky lines on the left hand but strong on the right, it means that the friendship is built on weak foundation and you are hoping for a lot more than it can, or is likely to, deliver (Figure 6.5).

It is important to realise that such lines do not always represent sexual love. I had strong affection lines on my hands which represented the births of my children. A mischievous friend pointed out to my husband that I had a strong one on my hand for a relationship that should have happened five years ago. The line actually represented a horse that I bought for my children. That animal pushed as many buttons as any human relationship might have done – and still does; added to which I was knee high in horse manure every day, wondering what on earth I had let myself in for.

You can't escape the truth about yourself when you look at your hands. We live in a time when personal fulfilment is seen as paramount, and many relationships are broken up in pursuit of it. There is a current ethic about relationships that if each partner fulfils him- or herself and breaks away from the relationship in the process, then everyone concerned (children, friends, family) will experience a knock-on improvement in their lives. Whilst I have found it sometimes to be true for joint concerns such as finances, work and love, that isn't the story told on the hands for a partnership break-up where children are involved.

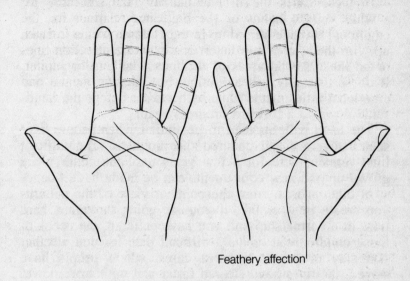

Figure 6.4

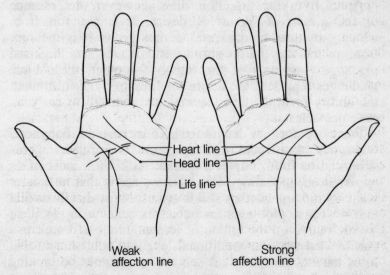

Figure 6.5

In these cases the lifeline usually runs smoothly for a while on the hands of the breakaway partner but the emotional carnage stirred up in the children seems to catch up with them, creating distortions in future affection lines or on the financial areas of the fingers of Sun or Jupiter. It doesn't usually last a lifetime but massive mental and emotional adjustments have to be made before the hands settle down to a forward progress again.

The hand patterns tend to be similar when people have stayed together and endured the problems. The difficult lines remain there for a few years until the children are grown up and new adjustments can be made.

In other words, from the point of view of the patterns you create in your life, if you are going through a hard time in a partnership and you have children, the needs of those children can create a difficult path for you whether you stay or leave. In most cases, where people have stayed, the lines have cleared faster and with more power – a sort of bonus for putting the children's needs before their own.

Apart from the affection lines, however, the essence of the mount of Venus is desire. It is the soil from which our most fundamental desires grow. It is the root from which the thumb springs and is, in fact, the third phalange (segment) of the thumb. Together, these three phalanges represent the desire for life, love and fulfilment, the ability to fulfil these desires, and the will to carry on over obstacles.

For most of us our desires for love are rooted in babyhood when our close bond with our mothers fulfilled, or was supposed to fulfil, our every need. As babies, most of us experienced unqualified love and we knew that no matter what we did, our parents still loved us. Many therapists feel that we cause problems for ourselves because in the West we are reared on the notion of romantic love and seek in a partner that same unconditional love and nourishment that most parents give us. It is felt that we should be seeking more adult relationships which recognise our partner as a separate human being, and that we should be whole and independent in ourselves.

All this is very fine and worthy, but I believe that we can have both. We can be independent, successful adults and also have a deep, unqualified loving bond with a partner. It can be intensely romantic and erotic as well. Of course, the achievement of such a bond isn't going to be plain sailing all the time. It might even be full of problems. But if deep, romantic, committed love is what you want and you are patient and unwavering, deep, romantic, enduring love is what you will get. Here's how:

Step 1

Take a piece of paper, but before you write anything on it think very seriously about the kind of love you want. What sort of lifestyle do you want to lead with your lover? What do you want him or her to be like? What sort of sex life? If you are in a long-term relationship think back to the time you met. What were your ideals then and how far did your partner seem to fulfil them? What is the state of your relationship now? If it has veered a long way from your ideal, what can you do to bring it back on course? It is rare for one partner to be the sole cause of difficulties. At some level you will have colluded, co-operated or even driven them to it.

Now begin to write about what you want in your love life. Free-associate as you go. Don't hold back. This is an exercise which you can tear up if you want to, so write at your most uninhibited. Let your true Venus self state what it wants.

Step 2

Take another piece of paper and, again, before you write anything, think very seriously about your love life. Go back to your earliest longings about love, to your first crush, then go right through all the loves and relationships to the present time. What was wrong with all these former loves? You didn't end up with any of them, so something wasn't right for you. Did any of them dump you? If so, why do you think that was and how did it make you feel? Did you dump any of them? If so, why did you do it? Did anyone betray you or treat you badly?

Now that you've loosened up your memories and emotions a bit, begin to write. Free-associate and jump about if you want to. The important thing is to let your thoughts flow and express your deepest feelings.

Step 3

Look at your thoughts from step 2. How often did you come out hurt or disappointed? How often did you feel you weren't attractive enough, sexy enough? How often did you feel guilty or a cad?

Well, it isn't true. They were simply the wrong people for you, but those thoughts about yourself will be affecting both your current and future love life.

So close your eyes now, and again take your thoughts back to those old relationships and begin to tie up all those loose ends. See each one ending in love and harmony with good feelings on both sides and recognition that you shared something but agreement now to move on happily. If you incurred displeasure from other people by the ending of an old love – say a parent or relative – settle this now. It was nobody's business but yours and the ex-beloved's and you don't need to carry it around with you.

If it was a marriage and there were children, this is an exception. See yourself giving all your love and tenderness to your children, no matter how angry or confused they may seem to be. See yourself sorting out some of the unspoken difficulties. Put yourself on the line and allow them to give you hell. See yourself forgiving yourself, them and your ex-partner. Make a mental note of any insights you get when doing this. There may be something that you can profitably act upon.

Step 4

Look at all the negative comments you have made in step 2 and put a circle around them. Now turn each one into a positive affirmation and write it down. You may get a list that looks fairly silly at times, but it nevertheless represents a deep part of you that has found it a stumbling block. For example, for women, your negative list might be something like this:

- Roy preferred Jane to me. Jane is prettier.

- Kathy took Mike off me. I hate Kathy.

- I gave Jim up and you'd think I'd committed a murder. All his friends gave me the cold shoulder.

For men, your negative list might be as follows:

- Jenny went off with Matthew who was a brilliant footballer. He's got bandy legs and I never understood what she saw in him.

- Linda was everything a man could wish for, beautiful, talented, sexy. I just couldn't match her lifestyle.

- I just couldn't stand Cheryl's possessiveness. I couldn't go anywhere without her checking up on me. It was like being married without the sex.

You need to get to the core of your negatives to see what rotten ideas about yourself you've ended up with; and to begin to heal these you need to turn all the negative statements into positive affirmations. The above lists would be turned round like this:

- I am not Jane. I am unique and attractive in my own way. Hope Roy enjoyed her.

- Kathy was a cow but I let that go. Mike would never have been right for me anyway.

- It was OK for me to give Jim up. I wasn't married to him and I'm better off without that sort of hassle.

- It doesn't matter what Jenny saw in Matthew. The more mature I am the more attractive I become.

- I had a choice: I could either have created Linda's lifestyle for myself and then pulled girls like her, or I could look at who I really am and realise there is a perfect partner for me.

- Cheryl made me feel a cad because I wasn't doing what she wanted. It is OK for me to live as I want and to have a partner who enjoys me and her own life.

Step 5

Look at your positive statements from step one. This is your ideal love life and you want to rev it up. The quickest and easiest way to do this is to make affirmations using the present tense and using your own name. The mind only acts on information in the present and you are here implanting ideas to correct negative ideas that have crept in over the years. For example:

1. I———am now creating a deep, loving, sexy relationship.

2. I———deserve a deep, loving relationship.

3. I———am ready to accept a deep, loving relationship.

4. My lover adores everything about me.

5. I———am the absolute ideal person for my lover.

6. I———am everything to my lover.

7. There is nothing that can come between us or separate us.

8. I——am willing to work out any difficulties.

9. I——am willing to give——the benefit of the doubt.

10. ——and I are talking to each other and resolving our difficulties.

11. I——am worthy of——'s deep love.

12. As much love and tenderness as I give, he/she returns it.

13. ——is a lovely person and I respect him/her.

14. ——feels this respect and glows with the love I have for him/her.

15. I acknowledge——'s right to live a life independent of me. This only makes us closer.

16. I give——as much freedom as he/she needs to fulfil his/her life. The more freedom and fulfilment he/she experiences, the deeper our relationship and the greater the benefit to me.

17. I——give——all the support he/she needs and he/she gives everything to me.

Getting Close without Sex

Because love and sex is one of our basic drives, the following exercise is to give yourself the experience of total acceptance at all levels. It is based on a yoga technique – the word yoga meaning union – and can be done with children, parents and friends. It is especially effective when done between lovers, although some macho men might resist the idea at first. Although it may seem deceptively simple, it is in fact a powerful, uniting exercise.

You need to find a time when you can both relax without interruption for twenty to thirty minutes. Get your partner to lie down on a bed or sofa, or even the floor if you will both be comfortable this way. He or she should loosen any tight clothing and relax, while you need to sit comfortably in a position where you can observe the rising and falling of your partner's abdomen as they breathe.

Your partner may feel a bit self-conscious at first so give yourselves time to settle and encourage him or her to breathe as naturally as possible, trying not to think about it or control it. Now as you sit watching them, notice the way they breathe. Notice their diaphragm rising and falling, and very gently allow your own breathing to fall into the same rhythm. As he or she breathes in, you breathe in. As he or she breathes out, you breathe out. Keep this up until you feel that you are breathing in harmony.

After a few breaths like this, it is quite common for people to become self-conscious and to lose the rhythm. Just focus again on your partner's diaphragm and gently allow your breathing to follow theirs.

It is also quite usual to get a 'high' as you realise the extent of your harmony and this can cause you to close your eyes or disconnect from your partner. Again, just focus on their diaphragm and allow your breath to move in harmony with theirs.

When you feel that this is flowing smoothly, inhale together with the same rhythm. As you both exhale, make the sound AAAAH as if a deep sigh is being released from your body. Let this sound drop deeper with each exhalation as you let go and release more deeply until it seems to vibrate up from the very roots of you. Your partner continues to breathe silently but your exhaled AAAAH must be loud enough for them to hear. They may fidget or open their eyes when you first do this but will quickly settle again.

Gradually, your partner begins to experience the sound of your out-breath as if it is theirs. Keep this rhythm up until it feels that it has run its natural course. You may find that your partner has dropped off to sleep or is snoring away. This is a good sign. It means that they have relaxed deeply.

During the course of the exercise you will experience your relationship in a deeper way. Some people feel an overwhelming sense of peace. Others have noticed unexpected tensions and irritations surfacing and quickly floating away with the rhythm of the breath. Problems that can become fixed in daily life often emerge during this exercise and are released as surface trivia to the much deeper relationship that is often taken for granted in a long-established partnership. It is quite usual for a sense of the erotic to arise but it is best to complete the exercise rather than rip all your partner's clothes off and launch into a full-blown lovemaking session.

Just try to stay with the breathing rhythm until you feel that you have done enough.

In effect you are breathing your partner's rhythm in your own body and in a subtle way it is more intimate than making love. You are paying closer attention to them than you may ever have done. You are switching off your normal daily awareness with its hopes, anxieties and irritations to become aware of the subtle closeness that your relationship really has.

Quite a few people have found this exercise so potent that they have incorporated it regularly into their lives and often as a prelude to lovemaking. Just play around with it and develop it as you like. If it becomes part of your life you will certainly discover new variations.

What to do if you don't have a partner

The next exercise is to focus this kind of subtle energy on yourself. Our Western society is very goal-oriented but this is often at the expense of our inner awareness. No matter how successful our lives may appear to be, most of us have an inner longing to be loved and approved of unconditionally by someone else and can feel quite depressed when this appears to be lacking.

The next exercise is a potent one on several levels. It is physically and emotionally healing whether you have a partner/lover or not. If you are feeling low where love is concerned it will begin to boost your energy, and if you are looking for love it can help to attract it into your life. You may find it helpful to tape this.

Attracting and Creating More Love

Sit or lie down somewhere comfortably and close your eyes, gently focusing on the flow of breath in and out of your body, the rise and fall of your diaphragm.

Now take your awareness to your body as a whole and for a few seconds allow yourself to see it as you think others see it. Some of you may be happy with this image; some of you may feel you are less than perfect. This image of yourself is a thought form that you are daily projecting into the atmosphere; it is creating the way people see you and how they react to you. It is time to put the blueprint straight.

See yourself now as beautiful and perfect. You may get an instant image of some kind of perfection or you may feel resistance. Either way, begin to allow a sense of loving your body to flow all over you. It is a magnificent machine, fine-tuned to organise every function, every second of the day and night.

See your body as perfect and lovely and also see other people looking at it in this way too. But being perceived as lovely is only part of what you want. You want love. So take a few moments to think about this. What is love for you? It is kind. It is forgiving. It is adoring. It is cherishing. It is tender. Is it anything else for you?

In fact, you already have all of this within you. It is within you to receive and it is within you to give. There are millions of people who all feel the same way. By tuning into this energy in yourself you begin to activate its ability to magnetise and attract its like towards you. Every atom and cell in your body vibrates to this energy. Try activating it with the following mental phrases. They may seem a bit over the top to some of you, but being in love *is* over the top and like attracts like. Take your awareness to the cells of your body and say:

- My cells are love.

- My atoms are love.

- My blood is the fluid of love.

- My bones are structures of love.

- My skin is porous and light with love.

- My heart beats with love.

- My lungs are bellows of love.

- My kidneys are purifiers of love.

- My liver detoxifies love.

- My brain understands love.

Now see your lover coming to you. If you already have one see him/her coming to you. If you are without a partner at this time, picture your ideal lover coming towards you.

Your lover is filled with love for you, caressing you, being tender with you, gentle with you. You are both receiving and giving love. Enjoy this image and add to it if you like. Continue until you feel you have done enough.

Results

David is a friend of ours and in his mid-thirties. He was an embittered ex-lover who had experienced several difficult relationships. He had become pessimistic about ever finding love and had thrown himself into his work. His health had suffered and he was on drugs for high blood pressure.

He was downright scornful of the above exercise but after dinner with us one evening he allowed himself to be 'conned' into it by me. He was surprised that he liked it and since I'd had the foresight to tape it as I'd taken him through the exercise, he took it home with him and began to use it.

He kept teasing me that Miss Right hadn't appeared yet but at his next medical check his blood pressure was down and his medication was reduced. He had an inkling that the tape had something to do with it and began to use it almost every day. Within three months his blood pressure was normal and, although his GP advised against it, he stopped taking the tablets. His blood pressure remained stable and this physical result brought about a subtle but profound change in him.

He is extremely attractive, a hunk in fact, but his abrasive manner often had even his friends on edge. This abrasiveness seemed to vanish. He became softer and more approachable and began to take more interest in the people he was talking to. Before, his conversation had been witty and intellectual, but now he seemed more rounded. Women were falling over themselves for him but he didn't trust them or himself.

Much as it went against his cynical grain, he asked me to give him 'the works' on love so I gave him all the techniques that I am giving you. He worked steadily with them for two months, and then met Ali in quite interesting circumstances. He was running for the London train back to Oxford. Ali, whom he had never met before, was running just in front of him. It was a Friday night rush hour and the guard was waiting to blow the whistle. Luggage was piled up by the doors and as she ran for the step Ali tripped, falling heavily and grazing her hand on the strap of a suitcase. David, who was right behind her, gallantly bound her hand in a handkerchief and tended her with a drink or two until they reached Oxford.

The rest is history. Four months later they moved in together and are now planning to get married.

Gemma's Story

Gemma is 28 and believes that it is no longer a man's world but a young woman's. Although love was always on her agenda, she was not looking for a partnership, seeing it as hampering her plans for her future. At art college in her late teens several men 'got a bit heavy' and that made her all the more determined to put her career first.

After college she got a job as a junior designer in a fabric firm and set up in a small shared flat where she literally loved life – going out with her friends, entertaining them at home, enjoying the theatre and cinema.

I first met her when she was 22 and she was keen to improve her prosperity to the extent that goal-setting techniques, affirmations, power building and magnetising became a hobby. Her financial assets began to increase very rapidly.

Her flat-mate was totally different. Love for her was a top priority but her love life was a shambles. She was always on a high when it was good and on a low when it wasn't.

The point of Gemma's story is that men were fascinated by her. They loved her independence. Her flat-mate accused her of six-timing when she had six different boy 'friends' but to Gemma, friends is what they were. She just enjoyed them as people instead of getting torn inside out as her flat-mate did.

This kind of scenario lasted five years, during which time she spent several months travelling in Thailand, India and Hong Kong, studying silk fabrics and organising contacts which she used to set up a small business manufacturing garments made from Eastern silks.

She finally settled with Bernard, and I must admit that at first even I thought she had taken leave of her senses.

He was sixteen years older than she was, had been married with two teenage daughters. The ex-wife and daughters gave her a hard time but emotionally she flourished.

She had done some of the love exercises and knew that she wanted a steady man who would be faithful to her. Her career was still all-important. She didn't want a man badgering her to start a family and Bernard was tied up with his daughters. In fact, he gave her emotional security while she concentrated on her career.

Gemma's love lines revealed all this, including the line for Bernard, which was strong and clear on both hands. She really never had a problem herself. The people who gave her a hard time were her friends and suitors, who tried to force her into their own mould.

Gemma's story illustrates an important point. She is one of the most well-adjusted people I know. She loves all these kinds of techniques because they help her to uncover what she really wants, but, more significantly, because they have worked for her and she is successful, well-off and happy, she is an irresistible magnet to her many admirers.

In other words, once you get your life running as *you* want it and are happy in yourself, your love life will often fall into step with it because you are not needy. Many would-be lovers are put off by the hassling and depression that neediness can produce. So start working on yourself today.

What Is Happiness for You?

What would make you happy right now? Today?

If someone told you that in twenty-four hours you were going to be locked up for a year, what would you really love to do during your last day of freedom?

Go on, make a list.

When did you last do any of these things?

So, why are you wasting your life with mediocre pastimes?

Start to blast it up to full octane. Work on prosperity to give you more freedom.

Do you like yourself?

If not, what is it you don't like? Are you anxious or fearful? If so, many of the exercises in other chapters will help. Bach flower remedies are also good for healing mood and emotion. They are simple to use and you can find them at most health food shops and some good chemists.

Improving Your Health through the Venus Energy

Venus is associated with the parathyroid glands, the metabolism of calcium of phosphorus and thereby helps to keep the skeletal system healthy.

Eating plenty of seafood gives an abundant supply of phosphorus and also zinc, which fortifies the sex function and has long been regarded as an aphrodisiac. It has never been established whether seafood, especially oysters, actually enhances desire, but it certainly strengthens the sex glands and replaces zinc lost in ejaculation.

Venus is also associated with the kidneys, which in Chinese medicine are regarded as the root of the life force. Since the mount of Venus represents the root of all desire, leading to the will at the tip of the thumb, it has strong links with the life force in general. If you are lacking desire, you lack will, and as long as it lasts there is a seeping deadness in you.

To refresh the kidneys, it is a good idea to increase your intake of water. At least once a month, more if you can manage it, decide to drink two litres of water a day for a week, to help flush the kidneys and any excess toxins from the body.

Foot reflexology is also an excellent treatment to tone up the whole body. You can give yourself a do-it-yourself session if you have a small hard ball like a golf ball or those high-bounce ones you can buy in toy shops. Sit down with bare feet and imagine that the ball is covered with ink and that you have to cover your foot with this ink. With the ball on the floor, press the sole of your foot quite hard on to it as you roll it around.

The kidney area is in the centre of the foot about 2–3 centimetres from the instep – more if you have wide feet. Roll the ball round this area, pressing quite hard to tone the kidneys. It will improve the circulation to the area, improve the nerve supply and boost the energy channels. If the area is tender it means that your kidneys are under par, so do this for no more than five minutes maximum and then repeat the process every day until the tenderness goes.

This applies to any tender area on the foot. Repeat the treatment on alternate days until the tenderness goes.

Making a Love Cake

This is a bit of fun, rather like making a birthday cake, but instead of celebrating the achievement of another year, it is to enhance your love life.

Choose a recipe that you like – it doesn't even have to be a cake, you can make something simple like flapjacks if you prefer. Assemble the ingredients and get yourself in the right frame of mind.

If you are seeking to attract love, say aloud some appropriate love affirmations from step 5 on page 102. Write them out and stick them to your fridge, cooker and cupboard doors so you can see them while you work.

Now lighten your heart. All older cooks knew the importance of this, otherwise their pastry and cakes came out like bricks. You are an alchemist; all cooks are, and as the alchemy of heat works on your cake, so the alchemy of your thoughts is going to work on your love life.

When your cake is finished, decide whether you want to decorate it. It is better if you do and important that it is done with a light, buoyant, hopeful heart.

Most important, however, are candles. You can either

do this ceremony alone or include friends, but if the latter, just as in a birthday wish you don't divulge your desires to them. Light your candles, make your wish for love (and anything else you might want) and then blow them out.

Eat your cake knowing that in a subtle way you are assimilating into yourself your desires for your love life so that your mind has a clearer message about your love goals and can produce results more quickly.

Remember that, no matter what your love experience has been so far, if you want to improve it, you can. Remember, too, that if you happen to read your 'stars' for the week or month in a magazine or paper and they say that your love life is on hold or bad or whatever, don't believe it. Shut any such thought out of your mind and begin to work on what you want.

Your mind will always create better results than the acceptance of some 'prediction' unless that prediction is wonderful and supports your dreams. So trust yourself. Go for what you want. Your body and mind are a complete unit, so as you work on your mind there will be changes in your body and visible, verifiable changes on your hands.

7

Relationships and Communication: Mercury

What you can't communicate runs you.

(Walter Erhard)

Mercury is the planet nearest the Sun; it is the smallest in size and mass in our solar system. It always has the same face turned towards the sun so that one side is in perpetual sunlight, the other in shadow. This helps us to understand Mercury's rulership of Gemini, whose symbol is the twins. Typical Geminis are regarded as having these two contradictory faces – one minute being energetic and mercurial, the next flat and defeated.

In Greek mythology Mercury was the messenger of the gods, being depicted with wings on his heels, and communication is the essence of the finger of Mercury in palmistry. The major relationships of our lives appear on the mount of Mercury so that a marriage or established love partnership would show here and also the children we are likely to have.

The finger of Mercury is the little finger on both hands (Figure 7.1).

A good finger of Mercury will look balanced in relationship to the other fingers. It is often set low on the hand so that it looks short, but if you measure it, a good length would measure half-way up the first phalange of the finger of Sun (i.e. the section including the nail). When it

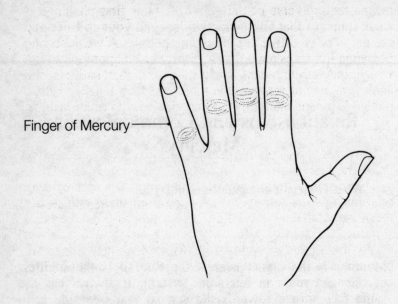

Finger of Mercury

Figure 7.1

is much shorter than this – say, measuring up to the joint connecting first and second phalanges or less, it means that you may have a problem with communication which could affect your relationships, both personal and professional.

A long first phalange means that you use your talents well to achieve your goals and probably have a lot of charm and 'gift of the gab'.

An equally well-balanced second phalange indicates a mind that communicates in a logical and practical way such as a lawyer, a doctor, a scientist or an accountant.

The third phalange represents the way we communicate and relate to the world, our feelings about our life on this planet in relation to others. A strong third phalange indicates an independent outlook which cannot tolerate restriction. Such a person would not work well for others.

If any of your Mercury phalanges are relatively weak, it

means the converse of the above. If your first phalange is weak it means that you lack confidence in your abilities and are not very effective at influencing people. A weak second phalange indicates a woolly or disorganised approach to life which inevitably means frustration and that success and achievement are much slower. A normally balanced third phalange means that you give and take well in relationships, but if it is weak it reveals a personality that can be exploited by others.

However, none of this is that serious. You can change it for the better.

The marriage lines – or partnership lines since many long relationships do not have the legal stamp these days – are the horizontal ones travelling across the cusp of the hand (Figure 7.2).

You may have more than one. If so, the earlier ones are bound to have breaks in them, or just fade into nothing,

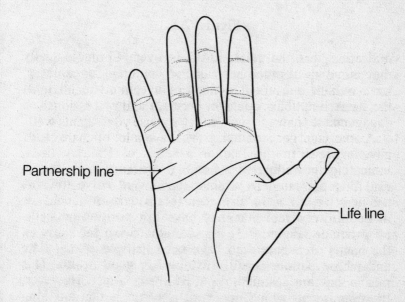

Partnership line

Life line

Figure 7.2

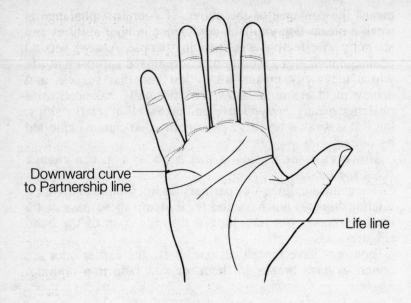

Downward curve to Partnership line

Life line

Figure 7.3

indicating that the relationship is over. Chronologically they move up from the heart line so you may, for example, have a faint one about a third of a centimetre up from the heart line. This could be your first love or a broken engagement.

A marriage or partnership which breaks up will either have a break in the line or a series of feathery lines, indicating the fading of a bond. If a partner dies, this is usually represented by a sharp downward curve towards the heart line. I have also seen this pattern on the hands of people who feel that they have lost position or status by marriage (Figure 7.3). In addition I have seen this on the hands of people who have been married a long time and whose partner is still alive and in good health. This means they are destined to outlive their partner. However, the premise on which my work is based is that anything negative can be changed and has been proven to change once restrictive thought patterns are uprooted. If your partner is holding life-shortening thoughts, these can be rapidly altered so that the lifeline lengthens, and health and longevity improve.

Right and Left Hands

You may discover that you have a break on a marriage line on one hand and not the other. If it is on the right hand but the left line is clear and well marked (Figure 7.4) it means that the relationship has all the qualities to endure well but that one of you has decided to end it. This is happening a great deal at the moment as people seek personal fulfilment and refuse to ride over rough patches.

If the break is on the left hand but not the right, it means exactly the opposite: that the relationship is not a bed of roses but the couple are sticking with it.

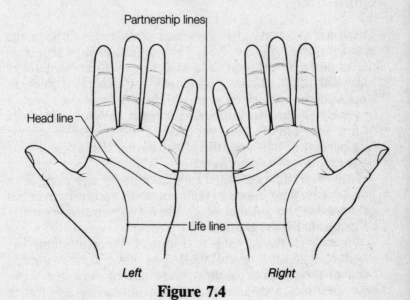

Figure 7.4

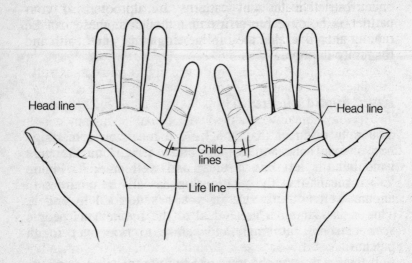

Figure 7.5

Child Lines

These are the vertical lines which often cross through the
marriage lines (Figure 7.5). They do not always represent
the number of children you will have but can sometimes
represent other children to whom you are close such as
stepchildren or beloved grandchildren. I have even seen a
few cases where an unmarried woman has had a plethora
of fine lines only to discover that she is a teacher or a nurse
in a paediatric unit and, therefore, has an important impact
on a number of young lives.

However, the most usual indication is for any child lines
you have on your hands in your late teens and early twenties
to represent the number of children you were biologically
or emotionally programmed to have.

When you reach your mid-thirties, the patterning has
often changed to reveal what you have done with the
original programme. A short blunt line or very fine wavy
one often indicates a termination or miscarriage. A strong

straight line indicates a male energy but this can also turn out to be a very career-oriented and determined girl. A finer, straight line indicates a feminine energy but this can also turn out to be a sensitive boy.

Quite often now, women in their early to mid-forties still have lines representing unborn children. These are children they still want to have and, indeed, may go ahead and have. But when a woman finally gives up on the idea of having any more children, these lines tend to fade. Of course, men have child lines too and the same rules apply. I have seen a good number of men who have had a vasectomy but there is still a child line on their hands. It can mean that although they have cut their natural reproductive life short their partner wants another child, or that they have a new partner who wants a child.

Whatever the case, a strong child line represents part of your psyche that wants to reproduce. If this is biologically impossible, that reproductive urge needs to be channelled into something else that can be absorbing and fulfilling.

Some child lines have a break in them (Figure 7.6).

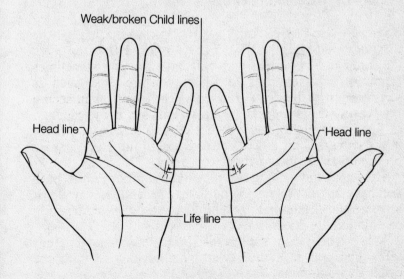

Figure 7.6

Often the section nearest the heart line is thin, and after the break it starts thin and gradually becomes stronger. This is usually found on the hands of parents who have separated or divorced. It means that the child has taken the separation badly and, for a while, the child's life lacks direction. Sometimes the lines never fully recover, but when a great deal of love and attention has been given to such a child, I have seen the lines strengthen.

One final point about the lines on the mount of Mercury (see Figure 1.1). Some people have one or two strong vertical lines a little further over from the child lines (Figure 7.7). These indicate a gift for communication, especially if they reach down as far as the head line. Such lines indicate the ability to make sense of difficult concepts and to put them across to other people. If you have such lines you either are, or would be, happy in a profession which uses these skills such as writing, journalism or teaching.

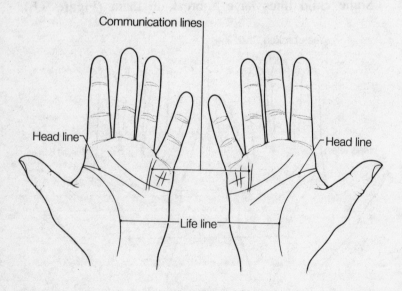

Figure 7.7

Reinvent Your Relationships

Your first relationship was with your mother and possibly your father. In order to clear the path for a brilliant love life and trouble-free communication in your relationships, we have to start here.

Arrange a quiet fifteen minutes or so, sit down and close your eyes. Breathe steadily for a minute or two, becoming aware of the air going in through your nostrils and the rise and fall of your abdomen. You have probably become quite adept by now at taking your memory back to your earliest months, and this time you are going to go back to your earliest memory of your mother.

Even if it's only a fleeting vision of yourself in a cot or at her feet or in her arms, keep breathing steadily, your abdomen rising and falling, as you allow your mind to access these early pictures.

Try to see a bit more now. You may get an intense flash of colour, of unwrapping a present perhaps, or you may see your mother's hairstyle and face looking much younger. Keep breathing and remembering as much as you can.

Now do the same thing with your father. Try to recall your earliest memories of him. Picking you up perhaps, or playing rough and tumble?

How do you feel? Secure? Contented? Is there anything here that is not peaceful or good? How do you feel about your mother? Your father? Are there any seeds here of the relationship you now have? Do you feel like a little prince or princess who is in total control of his or her world?

Keep breathing and remembering until you feel you have done enough.

Now, still with eyes closed, relax and think about any insights you may have had.

Did any of your recollections make you aware of something that has caused certain assumptions later? A father who was away a lot, perhaps? A working mother? A nanny? A childminder? Were there any restrictions? Or was it totally wonderful and easy, and later life seemed hard by comparison?

It is important to remember the good things from this time and to see yourself as the powerful, independent being you initially were. It is also important to forgive any negative ideas now. They are over and you can replace their energy in your memory banks with the quality you really want.

See your life as a steady stream of this good, hopeful, powerful energy. See it flowing from your earliest months to your life now. What events and people have got in the way to block it? Could you have done things differently?

Look at those people and imagine yourself handling it differently so that your life was smoother and more fulfilled.

By doing this, you are actually beginning to give your mind new instructions. You are giving it new guidelines to help it to act differently in the future. So give your mind as much time and detail as you like.

Sorting Out Current Relationships

Step 1

Take a piece of paper and write down the names of the people you have the most difficulty with. Your finger of Mercury may show good communication skills, but you will probably have several people with whom you have difficulty.

Step 2

Take the name at the top of your list and think about that person for a minute or two. What annoys you about them? Do you tell them how you feel? If so, how do they react? If you don't tell them how you feel, what is stopping you? Good manners? Fear?

Step 3

Whenever a relationship is irritating you it is usually because that person does not seem to accept or acknowledge you or what you are trying to say; so you can do either of the following exercises or preferably both.

(a) Take another piece of paper and write down what you would like to say to this person. You can make it as aggressive and abusive as you like but get all your feelings out. If the energy is flowing well you begin to feel angry or upset. Allow this feeling to express itself in words on the paper until you begin to feel better and more on top of the situation. If you get stuck and feel that you don't want to write any more, there is something in this relationship that you are refusing to see and should move on to step (b).

(b) I've mentioned this technique briefly before, but here it is part of a systematic approach to release you from your relationship blocks.

Get a pillow, put it on a chair and sit yourself opposite. This pillow represents the person who is not listening to you, who is not acknowledging you, who makes you furious, or worse, powerless. You can pin a photograph of this person to the pillow if you like, to help you make the connection more fully.

Now forget that this is a pillow. It represents this person and you are going to tell them how you feel. You are going to explain your unhappiness and frustration and why they drive you mad. You are going to tell them how you expect them to behave and that you want some respect and acceptance or whatever else is appropriate.

If doing this makes you angry, take the pillow and punch it or shout at it, or wring its metaphorical neck. Whatever you feel coming up, do it to the pillow. We can't go round duffing people up in real life but our caveman selves have been bursting with this energy and if it is suppressed, it slowly kills us. So let it all out now.

When you feel you have done enough, sit back in your chair and relax. How do you feel? Purged of your feelings? Or still a bit frustrated? How much violence did you feel? This has been simmering away in your body, your nerves and cells and running part of your life. Decide to take at least one small step to alter the way you handle this relationship. If this person is not listening to you, withdraw some of your energy from them by saying to yourself that you don't need this. You are worth more. Breathe deeply.

You don't have to be rude or abusive to them. Simply know that you are worth better treatment, and as you acknowledge this, new opportunities and better relationships will begin to open for you. Even this difficult relationship is likely to improve.

The pillow exercise works equally well for a relationship that has gone, whether it is the end of a love affair or a bereavement. It is very common for people who have lost someone close to feel that many things were left unsaid, and this technique is a good vehicle for expressing this. Your feelings are likely to be ones of sadness, and silly though it may seem, hugging the pillow as you begin to express them can be both cathartic and therapeutic.

Carolyn's Story

Carolyn was an only child and had a very difficult relationship with her mother, who had been a devoted daughter herself and expected very definite duties from Carolyn. The major difference in their lives was that Carolyn has an executive career and her mother has never worked and is now a widow. As a result she did not understand the demands of Carolyn's work, and resented it. Every year Carolyn was expected to spend her holidays with her mother. Since she travelled with her job, she felt that that would have to suffice for her own independent travel, so she resigned herself to giving up all her holiday time.

Each year before the holidays, Carolyn developed eczema on the Mercury (little) finger of her right hand, indicating that she was blocked in the conscious day-to-day dealings with her mother and that she was allowing herself to be exploited.

After doing this exercise she was enraged not only at her mother's demands but at herself for being such a wimp. So, instead of giving all four weeks of her annual holiday to her mother, she took off to Greece by herself for a fortnight. Her mother called her uncaring and unfeeling; so Carolyn carefully explained that this was exactly how her mother's behaviour appeared to her.

I wish I could say that Carolyn's mother became all sweetness and light right away but, in fact, her attempted manipulations got worse. The difference now was that Carolyn was not only doing what she could for her mother, she was also beginning to put herself more firmly into the equation and could see just how difficult her mother could be. It salved her conscience and also released more energy for her own life and the eczema on her little finger cleared up.

She began to see that her choice of an executive career had been to make herself as unlike her mother as possible and, as a result, she had shunned the possibility of marriage or a partner. The more she progressed with these exercises, the more she wanted to change her life and began to work on her love life.

Four years later she got married and Carolyn's mother now understands her daughter's life and can relate to it. Carolyn still works but her mother has settled down and begun to build a new circle of friends.

What To Do with Relationships That Won't Budge

Despite your best efforts you may still be up against a brick wall. The person won't see your point of view and you feel upset, wronged, guilty, frustrated or angry. Let's suppose that this is not a relationship you can walk away from. It is your spouse, your partner and you love them, but something is blocked in the relationship.

- He works late a lot. He is either a workaholic or you suspect something else.
- She's extravagant. She loves beautiful clothes and a lovely house. She's overdrawn on your joint account.
- She's got a parent fixation. She wants them around at weekends and you just want her.

The permutations are endless but anyone in a long-term relationship will have something at some time that drives them crazy. So, first of all go through steps 1–4 and try to improve things.

If your partner still won't accept what you're saying – and I can guarantee that if it's a man and his sport/friends/work are involved, it's unlikely – then forget it. Not the relationship. Just forget the situation and take a good look at yourself.

Most women I know, myself included, grew up with a romantic view of having a soul mate who would be our lives, our all. Unfortunately, most men don't understand this, except possibly the French, and we waste our time if we expect it. However, men tend to be much more deeply bonded to us than their behaviour would imply. So, if they're up to their macho bit, let them get on with it and make strategies to deal with it:

1. Be kind.

2. Each time he annoys or angers you, do something to enhance your own life.

3. Give yourself a treat.

4. Make affirmations to bring more of what you want into your life.

5. If you are working towards a goal (financial, work, more love), use the irritant in the relationship to create a sense of deservedness, of increasing independence and power.

6. Have loads of sex and be inventive.

7. Get a sex manual and try something new.

8. Use the breathing exercise in Chapter 6 (p. 103) if he'll let you.

9. Massage each other.

As for men who are having trouble with their women, the answer is usually very simple. Even if you are incandescent with rage or frustration, simmer down and listen to what she has to say. Lack of romance is often at the root of the trouble. Women don't like being snowed under with drudgery any more than men. A little tenderness and attention goes a long way.

If the Problem is not with a Partner

Use points 1–5 in the above list every time the person annoys you. Try forgiving them: not in the sense of seeing their behaviour as acceptable, but in order to cut yourself loose from it.

Close your eyes and imagine that you are drifting out to sea with this relationship weighing you down and preventing you getting ashore. Imagine that there is a knife or pliers to hand which can cut through the ropes or chains that are binding you. See this person swimming to shore away from you while you choose a safe and welcoming spot on dry land and float easily towards it.

This imaginary cutting process has an actual effect on the electromagnetic field which surrounds your body and can lighten you up emotionally.

If your problem is with a child, especially a teenager, then the only way forward is patience, perseverance and as much psychological wisdom as you can muster. Again, steps 1–5 will help to give you a sense of proportion.

Helping Children

If you have young children, the following technique is very helpful.

When they are asleep most parents go in to check on them. At this time, say some affirmations to them. Their brains are very receptive during sleep and their breathing rhythm will often change as you speak, or they will give a deep, releasing sigh. You can say things like:

- You are a wonderful boy/girl.

- Everyone likes you.

- You are getting better at school every day.

- You have a good brain and learn easily.

- You are paying more attention to your teachers.

Because you are using the second person 'you', it goes a long way to undo the damage created by spiteful children, harassed teachers and even sometimes, thoughtlessly, by you and other relatives.

Rooting Out Your Fantasies

Fantasies are images created by our imaginations, which can give rise to feelings of longing or desire. As long as they remain fermenting in our minds they are distracting us from reality and preventing us from getting the loves and relationships we really want.

The next exercise will bring your major fantasies to the surface and will help you to see and feel differently about your love life and relationships. You are going to write an imaginative piece about your fantasies in the framework of a story.

Don't think 'I can't write. I'm not going to do this,' and turn to the next exercise or chapter. We all tell stories all the time. Every time you relate an experience to someone you are constructing it in the narrative of a story. But this time you are going to do the same thing with something that hasn't happened to you – your main fantasy.

Take two or three sheets of paper – lined is probably best, but anything you have to hand will do. Don't write anything yet.

Sit for a few minutes – with eyes closed if you find this easier – and think about your main fantasy. It may be about a torrid love affair. It may be about a brilliant career or lifestyle. You are the main character; get as many details as you can in your mind about your supporting cast and the setting.

Now take a pen and begin to write. Put down the first sentence that comes into your head, no matter how bizarre, and begin to let the words flow, gradually introducing your fantasy and characters into the narrative. Write a story around this fantasy with a beginning, a middle and an end and let all your wildest dreams – erotic, of wealth, of ease and luxury, of changing the world for the better, of travel, or whatever it is that stirs you – be played out in your story. Really get your feelings into it. Write from the heart but allow your reason to give your fantasies the structure of a story. Introduce dialogue so that you are expressing what you want to say to your other characters and also have them expressing what you want to hear from them.

You don't have to finish this all at one go. Some people enjoy it so much that they take several sessions over it.

When you have finished

How has this made you feel? Fulfilled? Or frustrated? Most fantasies come from feelings of lack, and writing about them pulls them to the surface and gives them the beginnings of reality. However, this is only a start. The purpose here is to move you from wishy-washy inactivity to fulfilment.

So take a good look at these fantasies. What lack are they trying to fulfil? Is it love? Is it career? Is it money? Or a combination of several things? As long as they're fantasies they are actually like the image I gave you at the end of the last exercise. They are like weights to your body adrift in a sea far from dry land. They are stopping you getting on with your life unless you do something about them.

I am not suggesting that if your fantasies are of wild orgies with dozens of gorgeous people that you go out and start propositioning or making passes at anyone that takes your fancy. But such fantasies represent a repression in our sex lives. If you haven't got a lover then they serve a useful purpose temporarily, as long as you don't get stuck there. If you need a more fulfilling love life, decide what it is that is lacking and take the first steps towards improving it using these techniques.

If your fantasies are of a better career, again dreaming is fine as a start but when it becomes fixed as a fantasy – something that is in a never-never land – you are heading for frustration. So take some action today. What was your story about? Where was it set? Go and visit such a place as soon as you can – an airport, a hospital, a large company or whatever it happens to be. If you can't go right in, walk in and chat up the receptionist. Take away brochures. You may decide that this isn't what you really want after all but it will move you forward. Don't feel defeated. The next exercise will help you to move on from that. But first:

Jane's Story

Jane's father was a very wealthy man and her childhood had been spent in a lovely spacious house. She had had ponies and horses, lovely clothes and plenty of pocket money. But none of these had been provided by her father, who was constantly wrapped up in his work. All the luxuries of her life had come from her grandmother and when she had wanted to go to college her father had refused to pay for her. Her grandmother agreed with her father in the belief that a woman's place is in the home and wouldn't help with higher education either. She was like a gorgeous doll – pretty but mute.

She wrote several fantasies, all of which revolved around a wealthy man, quite often old enough to be her father. This man always became her lover and showered her with gifts, giving her everything her father hadn't. In every story her father violently disapproved of the match and each one ended with Jane figuratively sticking two fingers up to her father saying, 'There, I made it on my own.'

She found the writing exercise very liberating and realised that she was never going to get more from her father as things were. As a result, the actions she took were to isolate those things she wanted from her father and work towards them herself. She made goals around finance and career and, although she was in her early twenties, arranged to go to university to study economics and business.

She was accepted on the course and a grant was arranged, so she was well organised for moving her life forward.

However, total healing came from a forgiveness exercise that I gave her in which she consciously tried to release her bitterness towards her father. To her amazement, her father did a complete about-turn and gave her a large amount of money. She had advanced so far with her life that she could have made it without her father's help now, but the forgiveness exercise completed and resolved her difficulties.

She never had any more fantasies about older men and money, has received her degree and has a happy love life.

This exercise helps to unlock many repressed areas around relationships and creativity. If you are doing it properly and really allowing your feelings to surface, it is a powerful tool for growth. If you enjoy it, use it often. It can lead to all sorts of new developments in your life.

Dealing with Defeat

In all our relationships and endeavours we can suffer

setbacks and sometimes these assume such monumental proportions that we become practically immobilised. The next exercise is something that can be profitably used for a good deal of your life and if, after a few times, you like it, I suggest you buy a notebook with an attractive cover.

Daily Development Book

Step 1

If possible, write first thing in the morning. Before you read the newspapers or switch on the radio or television, give yourself five to ten minutes to write *whatever comes into your head*.

You will have just emerged from sleep, hopefully refreshed, but we're not enlightened beings or saints so there is a lot of garbage kicking around our brains which can lie like a booby-trap waiting to trip us up. So write down your feelings or ideas. By writing first thing in the morning you are making sure that what you write is an unadulterated outpouring of your own mind before it has the chance to react to the ideas of others.

Some days you will feel good and your writing will reflect this. Some days you will feel terrible. Writing will bring it all to the surface and will often make you feel better. However, this is not the ultimate purpose. You need do nothing about it at this stage. Just write each day if you can.

Step 2

Some time after 6 p.m. or at bedtime, write in the 'Daily Development Book' again. Because at the end of the day you will be writing about events as well as feelings, you may prefer to have a separate book and use it as a kind of diary. Either way, put down whatever seems relevant about your day. It may be creative. It may be expletive. Just write as you feel. Again, you need do nothing more at this stage, but it is a good idea to keep up both of these exercises for about a week to ten days so that a flow can be established, but if you enjoy them – and many people do – continue for as long as you like.

Step 3

After the initial seven to ten days, find a time when you can peruse your notes without interruption. Read all the morning notes straight through and see what feelings they give rise to. Can you see a pattern in them? Are they revealing some dormant part of yourself? Are they expressing something that you have been refusing to look at because of pressure of work or family obligations or lack of confidence in your ability to achieve it?

On a fresh piece of paper write down carefully what these morning notes suggest to you and put the paper somewhere where you can refer to it on a daily basis. I fasten mine with a decorative magnet to the metal shelf support above my desk. Some people use a 'Post-it' note sticker.

You may not want other people to see it – in fact I always feel it is better if they don't. It is your communication with your own unconscious and input from others at this stage could thwart any emerging growth.

Use the same process with your evening notes. Read them all through and see how they make you feel. These are probably going to be much more practical, relating daily events, and you may be surprised at how much material they give you for seeing both what is not ideal in your life and what you really want to do about it.

Again, on a fresh piece of paper, note down the important points and put it together with your morning notes.

At first, when you glance at these two pieces of paper, although they state what you need to act upon, you may feel that there is a considerable gap between your life and the comments you have made. But it is easy: you do nothing more each day than glance at the notes. If you feel you must act on something, fine, if you don't that's fine too.

After several weeks

Has anything changed? Do you realise to your surprise that you have begun to do things differently? Many people do, but in any case, you now read the notes and use your more determined left-brained self to work out a course of action based on your notes. The kinds of things people do are:

- decide to be more organised with lists and plans of actions;
- move themselves from a rut and begin to look for more lucrative employment;
- do something about a difficult relationship;
- learn to say no;
- stop being so uptight and taking time off each day just for themselves;
- be appreciative of the love they have.

Your action plan may be very different and dynamic, but once you have initiated it, you will begin to enjoy a shift in your life. You can then either go back and start the process again – steps 1–3 – to uncover new levels of quality in relationships, or you can leave it for a while and come back to it if you feel you are stagnating.

Improving Your Health through Mercury

Mercury is associated with the central nervous system, the brain and respiratory system, and with the element of air. It is through enhancing our breathing, therefore, that we best develop the energy represented by our Mercury mount and finger and the function of Mercury in our lives and health.

Of course, we all breathe every second of the day and most health sections of magazines and exercise videos stress the importance of correct breathing. But, honestly, how many of us take that much notice on a long-term basis? It seems a lot of effort for not markedly noticeable results. However, any woman who has had a baby will tell you that correct breathing is a powerful tool. I well remember the birth of my second child, when the delivery was progressing well and very fast so they didn't bother to give me any painkillers – no pethidine, no gas and air. Absolutely nothing. I panicked and lost all my well-rehearsed breathing rhythm. One of the midwives took me in her arms – a literal hug – and told me to breathe with her – rather like the breathing exercise in Chapter 6 where I was breathing her breath. She helped me to re-establish the rhythm and I hardly noticed the discomfort. I just rode on my breath.

Ten years ago I became involved with the technique of Conscious Connected Breathing devised by Leonard Orr in the USA and have seen it dissolve emotional and physical blocks, thereby helping to heal arthritis, cancer and many other serious diseases (see 'Rebirthing' address on page 213).

To get started with good breathing all you need to do is to be in a position with your spine straight – either standing up or sitting down.

Step 1

Place one hand on your abdomen and one on your upper chest and breathe into the upper chest. Your upper hand should rise and fall with your breathing rhythm. Your lower hand should remain more or less still.

Step 2

Now take your breathing down to your abdomen. This means that your lower lungs are being filled with air. Your lower hand should rise and fall with your breath. This is giving your body much more oxygen than in step 1 and will nourish your cells and remove toxins.

Step 3

Keep step 2 going for a minute or two – it will probably seem like an eternity because our busy, chattering minds want to be doing something and the breathing slows it down. You can use this time to say any affirmations mentally. Decide beforehand what areas you most want to work on and repeat each affirmation ten times or so, or one affirmation per breath. As your breathing rhythm begins to control your body, your mind will be more receptive.

Step 4

Take your breathing back into your upper chest and connect the inhale and exhale so that when you take the air in you let it out naturally with a sigh but do not pause before the inhale. Repeat this twenty times. No more. Healing will begin to take place and a toxic release, but it is advisable to consult a registered breathing practitioner if you want to take this further. After a few professional sessions you are equipped to do the full process on your own. Addresses and telephone numbers are listed on pages 213–214.

Although it is difficult for most people to find time to do this regularly, it is a good idea at least once a month to spend some time each day for a week working on your current goals and techniques and working with the breath.

To begin to heal your love life and relationships, set aside an hour or so to work with the exercise 'Reinvent Your Relationships' (p.122) and 'Sorting Out Current Relationships' (p.124). These will lay the foundations for improvement and you can work on the other exercises as you feel prompted.

When you make a major breakthrough in a particular relationship or in your general approach to all relationships, you lifeline will strengthen and become clearer, new love lines may develop (see Chapter 6) and the relationship lines on your mount of Mercury may change. If you notice other lines changing or branch lines developing, this will show you what areas of your life are being affected by these new relationship developments.

Altogether, your life will feel happier, clearer and stronger.

8

Personal Power and Sex Life: Mars

It is better to have lived one day as a tiger than a thousand days as a sheep.

(Tibetan saying)

Mars, the red planet, is associated with war, taking its name from the Roman god of war. It is the planetary ruler of the zodiac sign of Aries and the co-ruler with Pluto of the zodiac sign of Scorpio. Both are regarded as strong, dynamic and potentially aggressive signs. However, the true energy of Mars is adventurous and pioneering. It is traditionally the first sign of the zodiac and as such associated with innocent energy and raw power.

Unfortunately, many of us have this innocent, raw energy dampened down at an early age and as a result stifle ourselves. Your hands will show you how this is happening.

There are two mounts of Mars and a plain of Mars, which are not always easy to assess in size and quality. They are to be found in the area generally bounded by the head line and heart line (see Figure 8.1), with the mount of Lower Mars to be found just inside the beginning of the life line.

If the mount of Lower Mars is full and fleshy it often means an overdeveloped hostility, while a flat, almost non-existent mount indicates the reverse: a meek and timid personality. Because this mount is inside the lifeline it can often reveal something of a person's early years.

If the head and lifelines are joined and chained at the beginning with small lines travelling down headline to lifeline (Figure 8.2) it means that you had a good deal of restriction in childhood, possibly were not allowed free rein to develop your natural creative/intellectual talents, and a certain amount of pent-up aggression can result from this. In women, this has often been suppressed and can sometimes indicate confusion between a sense of duty to parents and the driving force towards independence. It also often indicates that some dearly held ambition has been thwarted by upbringing. It is nearly always damaging but responds rapidly and successfully to techniques to develop full potential.

The mount of upper Mars is found on the outside edge of the palm beneath the mount of Mercury (Figure 8.1). Traditionally, it is associated with courage, and also stubbornness if it is well developed; and with cowardice and possibly disloyalty if it is weak.

However, I have found that its position as part of the

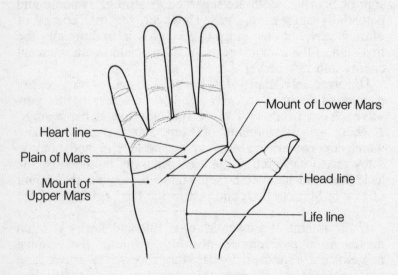

Figure 8.1

whole outside edge of the hand is important. It is part of the entire energy field containing the mount of Mercury at the top and the mount of Moon below. Mercury is, as we saw in the preceding chapter, to do with communication, the Moon to do with the subconscious mind. Because the lines and qualities of the mounts are created by the persistently held thoughts in our brains, you can see here the flow from the subconscious mind as revealed on the mount of Moon (see Figure 1.1, p.4) through to its conscious expression in Mercury. The mount of Upper Mars is in the middle. It is the sorting place between subconscious and conscious thought. It is the place where subconscious impulses are sifted before they reach expression. It is the melting pot.

The same is true for the plain of Mars, which is between the head and heart lines. Here the powerful, raw impulses with which the mount of Upper Mars deals are diluted into more civilised behaviour. The head line represents our mental qualities and creative abilities as we use them in the outside world. The heart line represents our emotions; so the

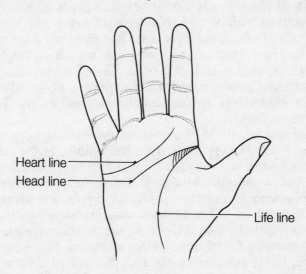

Figure 8.2

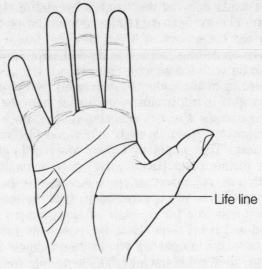

Figure 8.3

plain of Mars is a reservoir between the head and heart. It is another melting pot. No wonder anger and aggression can arise here. Mars represents that dynamic edge between our deepest impulses and what we actually do with them in the outside world. We often place lots of barriers and restrictions here – sometimes beneficially, but nearly always at the expense of our deepest energies and nearly always at a loss to ourselves.

So first of all, take a look at the outside edge of your hand – the side furthest from the thumb. Is the whole of that edge full and rounded (Figure 8.3) from the lowest edge near the wrist right through to the mount of Mercury? If so, it means that you have powerful drives and successfully fulfil them in a harmonious way. Is there a dip in the lower portions that fill out at the mount of upper Mars and mount of Mercury? If so, it means that you have a good, lively personality but feel the lack of creative force, sometimes frustratingly so if your mount of Venus is well developed.

If you have a full mount of Moon but it dips at the mount of upper Mars and Mercury, the position is reversed and you have an active, creative, intuitive mind but find it difficult to find expression for it. This is almost always an unfulfilling experience but can easily be changed.

Finally, if both mounts of Moon and Mercury are full but the mount of upper Mars is flatter it means that both creativity and the ability to express it are good but you are deeply blocked in doing either. You have abilities which are not used. You express yourself well and are probably popular, but in a superficial way. There is no harmonious flow between your deepest impulses and your daily life. Again, this can easily be changed for the better.

Quite often the plain of Mars (Figure 8.1) contains lines that are offshoots from the head line; or affection lines arising on the mount of Venus end there instead of travelling all the way up to the mount of Mercury (see Figure 1.1, p.4).

Offshoots from the head line (Figure 8.4) usually indicate

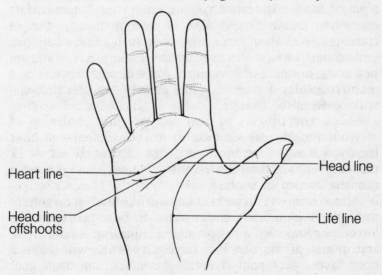

Heart line

Head line

Head line
offshoots

Life line

Figure 8.4

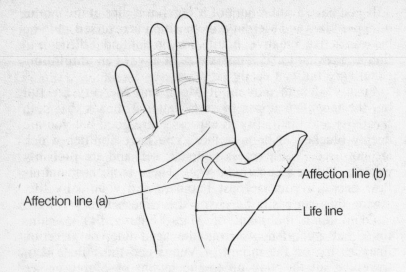

Figure 8.5

a period in your life when you are using your dynamic Mars energy to create a new way of earning money. People starting up new businesses often have such a line, or anyone embarking on a new creative endeavour. Similarly, if you are just about to start a new venture, you will probably see such an offshoot develop. Such a line usually indicates financial success from the change.

Check your fingers of Sun and the third phalanges of all your fingers (see Chapter 3) to see whether you have removed most of the blocks to your success. If not, work on the exercises for prosperity to give such an endeavour the best chance of success.

Affection lines that end in the plain of Mars have a similar meaning (Figure 8.5a). But, much to the disappointment of anyone having such a pattern, the relationship is unlikely to last; it also means that it is hugely dynamic, will unblock many aspects of your dynamic Mars self and open your eyes to new possibilities in both love and creativity.

A close friend had this pattern on her left hand and strong

clear affection lines going all the way to Mercury on her right. The clear right hand meant that she was seeing her present relationship as 'it'. She was deeply in love with him and called it a great love, the love of her life. He was younger than her, of a different and restrictive religion, and had a possessive family. As a result the love affair ended, despite her willingness to change her religion and do anything for him.

Surprisingly, she wasn't broken-hearted. The love was so intense and so total, she felt grateful for having experienced it. Like Tennyson, she felt it was better to have loved and lost than never to have loved at all.

The line on the left hand, which actually curved round in the plain of Mars and descended back to the head line, represented the true pattern of this affair (Figure 8.5b). As a result of her love for this man she had absorbed many of his creative interests, which were mainly writing and foreign-language films. She was a considerable linguist herself and decided to go to Paris, where she taught English as a foreign language and also wrote a novel based on the love affair. Although it was published, it wasn't a huge seller but it opened her world. She began to write romantic novels. They weren't the highbrow works that would have made her former boyfriend keel over in admiration, but they are very successful and she is now very well off.

She also met Pierre, a high-ranking executive in an industrial company. It wasn't the soaring, hopeless passion of the earlier love but was rounded and real. She is now married to him and lives in the wooded hills near Versailles.

She knows that but for the early love she would never have had the courage to go to France to work on her own. It was as if she travelled on the former love energy; and it opened up her yearning to travel and to write.

I kept vaguely in touch – Christmas cards – with the former lover. On his hands, the love lines representing my friend were wavy and insubstantial, meaning that the affair wasn't really going anywhere for him. His subsequent life hasn't gone anywhere either. He never married and has had a succession of jobs, trying, in his spare time, to write. Nothing has come of any of it except his devotion to his parents, brother and sister. Of course, he never involved himself in the techniques I am giving you. My friend did. You can too. Here's how.

Uncovering Your Own Dynamic Energy

As in the first exercises of several of the other chapters, if you want to reinvent your life you have to go back to the beginning to unravel the knots that are thwarting it. You may find it easier to put this exercise on tape.

You will need an uninterrupted fifteen to twenty minutes where you can sit or lie down and relax. If you feel tension anywhere in your body, try first to relax it, then tense the muscles up as much as you can and then let go. Breathe a few times into your lower lungs so that your abdomen rises, and close your eyes.

You may, by now, have devised your own way to travel back across the years to your babyhood. If not, take your awareness back to your earliest memories at about the age of eighteen months to two years. You need to go back further still; so just relax into your memories and take your thoughts back to the time when you were one year old. You would have been crawling around by then and probably even walking. You may have a vague recollection of this. If so, rest with the memory for a few seconds and then take your thoughts back even further, to the time when you were six months old. You probably had a rattle and a favourite cuddly toy. You may still possess one of these from that time or have seen a photograph of yourself; so try to make the link between your adult self and your six-month-old self, trying to recall the movements of arms and legs that you would have been exploring.

You may not make what you feel is a real contact. You

may not see anything or feel anything, but memory *is* there and by making a conscious effort now you *will* make some kind of contact – a fleeting sensation perhaps, a flash of insight or memory. At this stage in your life some of the ground rules were being set by your parents or carers and you would have begun to learn their approach to life. They may have been easygoing and allowed you free rein to kick and rattle, or they may have had a rigid timetable imposed perhaps by work so that you may have been put into your cot or pram for daytime naps whether you wanted them or not. You were learning dependence and helplessness.

Of course, this is necessary because we *were* helpless, but some of us learned that it was easier to play this game than to risk upset. So take six or seven deep breaths, taking the air all the way to the bottom of your lungs, then let it out again and see your cot. Was it a happy place to be or did it feel like a prison? You may now get flashes of other memories from an earlier or later time. This is fine. Your mind is trying to show you some of the significant events that shaped your feelings and ideas.

Keep breathing rhythmically. You may suddenly notice that you stop breathing or are breathing very shallowly. This is a sure sign that you have hit an emotional stress and if you just breathe lightly and gently you may discover what it was. Recall any of the things you know about that time to help you. Perhaps you remember the way the room was decorated, the colour of the carpet or some other kind of floor covering. These will help you to deepen your recall.

By now you should have made some sort of contact with your three-month-old self. There may be no consistent picture, just a vague array of sensations. That's fine. Whatever you are feeling or seeing is some sort of contact and as much as your mind wants to see at the moment.

Is there something about this period you don't like? Or maybe it was wonderful and you have a sense of unease about things that came later. Hold this sense of self for a few seconds and affirm now that you were embarking on a great adventure and that you're going to recreate the scenario. Anything that was uncomfortable, examine now and gently erase it, overlaying it with a sense of peace and also adventure. You see, these are only memories now but you made decisions then that are still affecting you in your present life.

When you feel you have done enough, sweep your awareness over the next three to nine months of your life to the time you were nine to twelve months old. By this time you would have begun to crawl or walk. You would have grown muscles strong enough to support you. Your world would have expanded and you would have been thrilled at the new possibilities – most babies are unstoppable. But someone *did* stop you. Someone would have put gates at the tops of stairs and said 'no' when your fingers got near electric sockets or when you tugged on the lead of an iron.

They were right to say no, but how did you register this? Did your little brain process it as just a no for these particular things or did it begin to be fearful of a lot of things? Recall this now. Many people who do this exercise see themselves as still strong and adventurous but as beginning to evaluate this person or persons who keep saying no and sweeping them up into the air away from trouble.

Put the record straight now. That adventurous spirit may have started the long slow process of quietening down to the point of loss of drive, and this is what you want to resurrect. See yourself rediscovering that childlike delight in new things, that desire to explore all possibilities.

You may know at what age you began to walk, so take your awareness forward to that time now. You have hauled yourself up and teetered forward to an almost undoubtedly admiring audience. You are very pleased with yourself. You're going to do a lot more of this. These big people think you're pretty smart.

Then you fall and hurt yourself. You cry and are comforted. Without realising it, this great new adventure is accompanied by almost certain anxiety and the possible beginnings of manipulation. Your every cry is comforted. These big loving people are your slaves and you enjoy their approval. This is another big milestone in thwarting the adventurous spirit and you're the one who is choosing it.

Later on, this approval is more difficult to get and at about one year to eighteen months old you have already built the framework which can cause a lifetime of sub-conscious disappointment. Scan your memory and begin to dismantle the framework that needs approval for your smallest achievement. Many a relationship has come unstuck over little things like this. You don't *need* anyone's approval but your own. This *must* come first. Anyone else's approval is secondary.

Recreate your baby memories. See yourself as making those first steps and tumbles and learning from them. Put the caring love and anxiety of your parents or guardians to one side. It's very nice of them but you've got big things to sort out on your own.

Rediscover your dynamic, adventurous spirit that got you to your feet in the first place, and allow it to filter through your memory banks into your conscious mind. It's still there. You've just overlaid it with all sorts of other maybes and oughts and shoulds related to other people and their view of your little world. Give yourself a few minutes to do this. You may not feel anything very much, but your intention is the key which will unlock it and allow it to be more active in your life again.

Finally, take your awareness to your first real adventure. You can walk now and you have wandered off. You didn't know you were doing anything wrong but somehow your carers are nowhere to be seen and you are having a wonderful time. You may have wandered streets away, exploring your neighbourhood. You may have been exploring the fields or woods or a pond. The grass and cow parsley could be swaying over your head. It's wonderful. It's magical. This is life. This is your world.

And then what happens? They find you. They tell you

off. They tell you that you're never to go wandering
off again. This wonderful world has been closed off for
you. It is dangerous to enter it again. And part of your
energy dies.

Uncover it right now. Resurrect it. Let it start to bubble up.
Remember how wonderful it felt and reinvent the scenario.
They didn't find you. You didn't get told off. You went
on enjoying it and went on further adventures. Reinvent
whatever adventures you like. Take them up to a later age.
Eight, say, or ten. Ignore the decisions you made about
adults and avoiding trouble. Imagine what you would have
done if you hadn't had that great block of 'You mustn't'
standing in the way.

Of course, we would never have learned about safety and
keeping ourselves out of danger if they hadn't done it, but
we are adults now and the energy can be recovered so that
we have the best of both worlds.

My sister had quite a lot of adventures when she was
small but the biggest one that we all remember was when
she was three or four. We lived on a farm then and she
vanished. My father found her in the bullpen, right up in
the corner with a ferocious thing called Ferdinand. She was
cuddling one of his front legs and he was nuzzling the top
of her head.

She was, in fact, in no danger at all. The bull recognised
her innocence. But after that, she learned fear and the
possibility of death near animals, and instead of more
adventures she narrowed her horizons and ended up as a
civil servant.

Rediscovering Innocence

Although this exercise starts off with a few recollections
of babyhood, it takes the process a stage further. For this
you will need a pen and paper.

Sit down somewhere comfortably and close your eyes.
If you are doing this exercise straight after the previous

one your brain will be tuned up, but if not, cast your mind back to your baby years when you were exploring things, picking up objects, smelling them, biting them, maybe sticking them up your nose. Adults were trying to tell you their names, were praising you when you repeated them; so you knew that it was in your interests to learn. You got cries of delight and hugs and generally got to feel you were marvellous.

But these were your first lessons in collective seeing. You were being taught to take your place in our culture but it was at the expense of your own unique way of seeing the world. We are now going to recapture this so that the unique, dynamic quality of you can begin to resonate more in your daily life.

Try and recall an early Christmas or birthday when you were unwrapping presents. Your senses would have been assailed by colours and ripping and crackling sounds. It was raw energy, raw sensation. Don't give a name to anything. Imagine things with no name, only the sensation.

See yourself in spring in a field of grasses, or a wood or orchard. See the fresh, bright green, the fragrant smell of the spring flowers. I am naming it, but now you go into it and see it, remember it or any other childhood memory that springs to mind.

This is raw, dynamic sensation and your interaction with it has no name. Naming it means thinking about it and takes away the sensation. So re-experience it. It is all there in your memory banks.

Continue with this for as long or as little as you like and then slowly open your eyes.

Look around you. Don't name. Just experience what you see and smell and feel and, above all, enjoy it.

Now select one object near at hand. It may be a cup or pen, a scarf, maybe something you are wearing. Without naming it, and without thinking about its name and associations for you, take your pen and paper and begin to write about it. Write what it looks like, its shape, its texture. What does it smell like? What does it feel like? Put it against your cheek where you can't see it so easily. What does it feel like now? If it has a picture or patterns or words on it, ignore their meaning and describe their shape, the way the colours make you feel.

Realise how, in our daily life in the rat race we have all helped to create and to which we all contribute in some way, we miss all this. We take it for granted and yet if you start to work with it through all these exercises you will automatically start to move your life into a new direction, or if you are fairly happy, you will, at the very least, add a new dimension to it.

You can extend this exercise by taking a picture and describing it without naming. Describe the colours and the shapes, but not your feelings which actually contain the meanings you have given these pictures. Most people get an almost gut reaction from seeing these shapes as they really are. We, as a culture, have given them meaning.

It is rather like the explorer who tried to explain to the natives that he had arrived in a ship. They went to the bay where it was moored but couldn't see anything. They had no word or concept for ship and the shapes of its hull and rigging were, therefore, meaningless. Because no thought form for ship had ever been imprinted on their brains they could not distinguish it from the trees or the sea.

Although our culture has many good things, by unquestioningly accepting everything we have been taught, we have also cut off our own dynamic, unique energy. With these exercises you are taking the first steps to releasing it.

Reinvent Your Sex Life

The Mars energy is raw and procreative. It is full of life force and relates to the gonads or sex glands. There are many excellent books and manuals that work on this in depth and detail, but the next exercise is to uncover and improve some of the possibly hidden elements of your own sex life.

There are two parts to the exercise: the first is passive and relaxing; for the second you will need a pen and paper.

Step 1

When you have a quiet fifteen minutes or so, sit down, relax and breathe deeply as before, relaxing more with each breath.

When you feel comfortable, cast your mind back to your first sexual experience. Relive this in as much detail as possible. Were you nervous? If so, what of? Your body? Taking your clothes off? Wondering what your partner was thinking about you? Or were you enjoying every minute of it? I hope so. But if not, now is the time to look at the anxieties you may have had and change them, because anything negative will have become associated with your sex life ever after, even with small things that you may have forgotten. Maybe it was too rushed or your partner turned out to be a disappointment – not necessarily sexually but perhaps letting you down emotionally. All this needs to be acknowledged and your feelings about it changed.

Recreate your first sexual experience in your mind's eye. Create it as you would have wanted it to be: hot and passionate, loving and fulfilling, or whatever else would have made it a perfect experience for you. If the partner dumped you afterwards, this can be very damaging even if the sex was brilliant; so release yourself now from any disappointments and see both the sex and the relationship in an ideal way for you. If you were dumped – and most of us are at one time or another – don't link this to your sex appeal. See the sexual experience as separate from the relationship. You may have had unrealistic hopes for the relationship but the sex drive is really sufficient in itself. In other words, see yourself really enjoying the sex and letting anything else about the person go.

Now move on to your next sexual experience if you didn't end up with the first one, and repeat the process. If the exercise begins to turn you on, that's absolutely brilliant

– the technique is working. In fact, I would recommend that you do to your body what you would like a lover to do to you and fantasise about your ideal as you do so. It will give your mind a blueprint for your love life and will help to bring it into your life faster.

Go through all your sexual encounters and reinvent them and the relationships they involved. You don't have to do this all at one session. Set aside time for it whenever you feel like it.

This exercise will not only help to improve your sex life. It will help to make you more relaxed and inventive.

Reinvent Your Life

We are all hemmed in by global thought. We are bombarded daily with the ideas of other people from the media, our families and friends; and this may be thwarting you. So take a paper and pen and list all the assumptions you have made about the general patterns of life. A typical example might be:

1. You are born.

2. Go to school.

3. Have sex for the first time.

4. Lark around until you have to become serious.

5. Have to get a job in order to live.

6. Maybe study to get a better job.

7. Be responsible or it causes trouble.

8. Settle down with a partner.

9. Have children.

10. Drift through into middle age.

11. Make more money and have a good time.

12. Get old.

13. Die.

Everyone will have 1 and 13. Pretty depressing, isn't it? All that dynamic energy ending up in a box or an incinerator. I shall deal more fully with longevity and living brilliantly under Saturn and Pluto. But for this exercise you are going to take your imagination on a short journey through your ideal life.

When you are born you have undiluted power energy. It is the pioneering spirit. It is vital and full of life. See it now as never being thwarted by adverse gravitational pulls from other planets, never being suppressed by the anxieties of parents.

What would you have done? What adventures have you suppressed in adulthood? See yourself now as an adventurous adult, exploring with the innocence and wonder that you lost as a child.

Take all or part of your list and work on it. Going to school, for example. What decisions did you make about yourself because of teachers or other schoolchildren? Look closely at the time when you decided what you were going to do – leave school and work maybe, leave school and go to college? Why did you make that particular decision? Is it really what you wanted to do? Was there some other dream that you never really expressed or that was stamped on?

Resurrect any vague dreams or longings and incorporate them into a new blueprint for yourself. What could you do now that could set the ball rolling, maybe as a hobby or recreation?

Go through all of your list, especially the areas your life hasn't reached yet, like middle or old age. With such areas you are in the powerful position of being able to create it exactly how you want, thereby thwarting social expectations of these years as being ones of diminished energy and enjoyment.

Each time you work on a section, use some affirmations

to 'fix' your ideas. Remember to write your first name and use the present tense.

Some sample affirmations are:

1. I————am vital and brilliant energy.

2. I————have come into the world to express this energy and do so now.

3. No planetary influence can upset me.

4. I————am more powerful than any influence over me. I erase all negative influences now.

5. My parents meant well but I now erase any negative advice.

6. My life is becoming daily more brilliant, inventive and interesting.

7. The older I get the more adventures I have.

8. I————am now reinventing my sex life.

9. I————now obliterate all negative ideas about my sexuality and allow myself to enjoy the sex life I want.

10. I————experience sex as fulfilling, fun and without harm.

11. I————can attract whatever money I like.

12. I————can create whatever money I need.

13. I————no longer resist the idea of being financially independent.

14. I————now enjoy playing around with simple exercises that make me wealthy.

15. I————now enjoy the idea of attracting more prosperity without slaving seven hours a day for it unless I feel like it.

16. Middle age is an exciting time to live.

17. My middle years are my best years yet. Older age is even better.

18. The older I am, the happier and more prosperous I become.

19. The idea of death was invented by someone else. I can go on living as long as I want.

This last statement may seem bizarre but most people tend to have a fixed idea of their likely lifespan, often based on family patterns. Once they have been given techniques like affirmation and visualisation to change these ideas, their lifeline grows and their health and general approach to life improves.

I have seen lifelines grow by as much as 3–4 centimetres, which represents approximately 30–40 years. So it is up to you. If you want to live longer and more healthily, root out your family ideas about age. I will give you more on this in Chapters 9 and 10.

Expanding Your Physical Limits

This exercise will help you to see how easy it is to move yourself further than your brain initially allows. It will give you a physical experience of expansion which will help you to accept the mental exercises more easily.

The example I am giving is from yoga, so make sure that you are wearing loose clothing. If anything constricts you at all, take it off. If you end up in your underwear, better still. You will be able to move more easily.

Now sit on the floor with your legs stretched out as widely as possible. Bring your left foot as close to your groin as possible as if you are going to sit cross-legged. Leave your right leg outstretched. At this stage, unless you are very supple your left knee is probably a few inches from the floor and you are just thinking to yourself, 'I'm not supple. I can't do this.' Well, you can.

Inhale deeply so that your abdomen rises. As you release the breath, lower your left leg a little more.

It went down another half to one centimetre or more, didn't it? And so you think this is your limit.

Inhale again deeply and on the out-breath relax and allow your left leg to go further. Again, you will notice that it has dropped another half to one centimetre.

Repeat the process until you feel you really can go no further. It's a fallacy, of course. You've got this idea that to go further is bound to break something or stretch it to impossible limits, but if you tell your brain that you can go just a little bit further each time and breathe into it – the breath helps the blood supply to the muscles and removes toxins released by the stretch – you can go very much further than you think.

Repeat the exercise with the other leg to even yourself up.

The point at which you decided to give up is your current physical edge – that point between progress and calling a halt. You have created edges in all areas of your life so see if, on a daily basis, you can extend your range further. This applies to anything progressive:

- learning new techniques;

- increasing your speed at routine jobs;

- increasing your physical speed and stamina in sports;

- improving your dexterity at picking things up and putting them down. You learned this as a child. Improve the relationship between your hands and the objects they handle or touch;

- walking as if there were air beneath your feet.

Above all, breathe deeply. Each time you are extending your range, ignore the negative thoughts and breathe into it.

Do the same with all your other goals where you are

extending your range. If you are aiming for an extra £1,000 for example, write some affirmations and breathe deeply as you write or say each one.

Dealing with Fear

Fear is the enemy of your dynamic Mars energy and is also the reason you have set certain limits to your activities and life. It is probably the most damaging emotion in your life, and for your dynamic Mars energy in particular.

Step 1

Take a piece of paper and list your main fears. Then list those things that you would like to do if you weren't afraid to do them. Don't rush this. Scour your mind for all those niggling doubts that actually have fear as their root.

Pam's list used to look like this before she set to work on them:

Fears

- Dying
- Getting old
- Getting ill
- My mother
- Horse-riding
- My mother-in-law
- Getting mugged
- Flying in aeroplanes
- Swimming in deep water
- Being stuck as a domestic dogsbody for the rest of my life.

Now as I have already explained, these fears are creating the lines on your hands. Fears of dying and getting old will adversely affect the length of the lifeline so that your fears begin to create your reality. Pam's fear of her strong-willed mother and mother-in-law created havoc on her head line. Instead of leading her life as she truly wanted – working part-time – she had both women on her back saying that her house was a tip (it wasn't; it just didn't get dusted every day as theirs did). Her mother-in-law also implied that she wasn't looking after her son properly. Pam's head line on her left hand went right across the palm in a gentle slope, indicating a creative career path. On her right it stopped short in the middle of the plain of Mars, indicating foreshortened dynamic energy. She was caught between her deep desire for progress in her own life and the duties that both mother and mother-in-law regarded as failure on Pam's part.

Step 2

Turn all your fears into positive statements.
Pam's were as follows:

1. My life is in my own hands. I can live as long as I like.

2. The older I am, the better life is.

3. I cannot become ill unless I accept the idea mentally. I now erase all ideas of illness.

4. I have allowed my mother power over me. I now release this. I am the leader of my life, not her.

5. It is OK to be scared of horses. If I really want to ride I can take easy, gradual lessons.

6. I owe my mother-in-law nothing. She has no rights over me.

7. The more I fear getting mugged the more I have a victim mentality. I release this now.

8. Flying is the safest form of travel. I now train myself to enjoy it.

9. I am the master of my body. I can swim well, so deep water is no different to shallow.

10. I now take small easy steps out of my domestic rut into the life I want.

Some of you may question the truth of statement number 3 about illness. If so, I highly recommend Louise Hay's *You Can Heal Your Life*. At the back of this she lists numerous illnesses and the states of mind that create them. Once you have accepted that your mind allows illnesses to take hold and you begin to make positive affirmations to correct this, you will notice a lengthening and deepening of your lifeline.

Step 3

Read your lists out loud and breathe deeply after each statement. When we are afraid we tend to hold our breath, so breathing fully as you state your changes is essential.

Step 4

During the next few days, if you come across a situation that makes you feel agitated, positively fearful or angry, breathe deeply and then make a note of it. You will probably come up with several more 'fears' to add to your list. You can then go through steps 1–3 to begin to change your life around.

Physically Improving the Mars Energy

As you already know, Mars is associated with the sex drive and with the urogenital system, adrenals (fight-or-flight glands) and kidneys. The following exercise is from traditional hatha yoga and is know as a *mula banda*, or root lock. It both stimulates and strengthens the urogenital muscles and will, as a result, enhance your sex life if used regularly.

In yoga it is an energy-raising process although only ashtanga yoga requires its practitioners to maintain the lock throughout all their yoga postures.

Women who have had a baby may be familiar with this exercise from post-natal classes, but as a yoga exercise it is potent for both men and women. You can do this exercise anywhere, standing up, sitting or lying down, even waiting in a bus queue. No one will know.

Step 1

Contract all the muscles of the pelvic floor. For women this will include the vagina and for both men and women, the anus. Pull in tight as if you urgently need to go to the loo and you're in a public place. This contraction is *horizontal*.

Step 2

Holding this contraction, start to pull it upwards at the same time as if you trying to pull the entire pelvic floor into the abdomen.

Step 3

Hold for a few seconds and then release.

Step 4

Repeat steps 1 and 2 and try to take the lift higher, using your imagination to take the energy all the way through your body. Don't worry if you get no further than your navel, you are achieving excellent results.

If you exercise regularly, use the *mula banda* just before and after you exercise so that you are reminded to incorporate it regularly into your routine.

If you don't take regular exercise, use it each time you take a shower or bath.

Remember, the dynamic Mars energy represents part of your most pioneering self. Using the techniques in this chapter will move you fast forward towards your deepest impulses and drives.

Check your hands every two or three months or so to see if changes are occurring in the Mars areas, especially in the space between your head and heart line (see Figure 8.1). You may also discover a lengthening and/or deepening of your lifeline see Figure 1.1, p.4), indicating that deep psychological blocks have been moved.

9

Lifespan and Money: Saturn

As dew is drawn upwards in rain to descend
Your thoughts drift away and in Destiny blend.
You cannot escape them for petty or great,
Or evil or noble, they fashion your fate.

                                    (attributed to a Maori)

Saturn is one of the most important planets in its effects upon our lives, after the Sun and Moon. Despite its distance from the earth, its size means that it has a large gravitational pull. The Saturn cycle is important in all our lives: Saturn takes approximately twenty-eight years to get round the zodiac so that when we are about 28 it is back in the same zodiac position as it was at our birth, and for most people this is a time of change. If you do not take the opportunities presented then, the Saturnine force will pile on the pressure until you do. There are also quarters of Saturn every seven years which exert smaller but significant pressures. To sum up, you will experience major movements in your life at the ages of 28, 56, 84 and 112. You will also experience significant developments at the ages of 7, 14, 21, 35, 42, 49, 63, 70, 77, 91 and so on.

Now, you may be wondering: if I am supposed to be able to reinvent my life, how do I deal with what seems to be a destined pattern? Well, the answer is, again, that your mind is certainly more powerful than the effects of this planetary energy, but my experience of Saturn over many years is that its influence is ultimately beneficial and benign. It is in our interests to work in harmony with it because it can lead us very slowly and surely towards our major goals.

Saturn rules Capricorn whose symbol is the mountain goat, the traditional quality of which is to climb slowly and inevitably to the top peak. Many of those born under Capricorn do, in fact, achieve success against the odds, but of course we all had Saturn in a specific position in the sky when we were born where its influence would have been more or less powerful. As with the other planets, you do not need to know this in order to discover how you are dealing with Saturn in your life: your hands will tell you.

The finger of Saturn is the middle and longest finger (Figure 9.1) and seems to dominate the hand. If you have a long first phalange (nail to first joint) it means that you have an interest in psychology or the paranormal and might even consider practising as a therapist. When the second phalange appears longer than the other two it indicates a strong practical mind, often revealing a scientific or

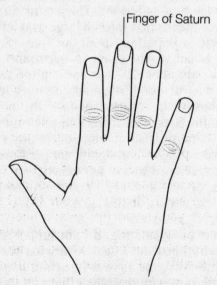

Finger of Saturn

Figure 9.1

mathematical ability. It also indicates an affinity with the earth and would be found on the hands of gardeners, farmers and anyone deeply concerned about ecological issues.

Traditionally the third phalange (nearest the knuckle) indicates a love of history, antiques and the established way of doing things – in other words a conservative mind. However, over the years it has become obvious to me that the Saturnine influence deeply affects our attitudes towards money. A full third phalange means, therefore, that you have the ability to amass money by tried and tested ways. A thin or wasp-waisted third phalange means that you are pessimistic about money in general and about your ability to become wealthy in particular.

Over and over again I have seen a significant discrepancy between right and left hands. The usual pattern is for the third phalange on the finger of Saturn on the left hand to be relatively balanced, revealing at least an adequate ability to make money for a comfortable life. The right-hand phalange is often the thinner or shorter of the two, meaning that your experiences and the beliefs you have chosen to hold have led you to think that money is hard to come by and goes faster than it comes in.

Money is one of the easiest and quickest things to acquire in your life; and because it so quickly improves our lifestyles, it has a knock-on effect in all other areas.

The other important aspect of Saturn on the hands are the lines of Saturn which travel up from the lifeline to the mount of Saturn beneath the Saturn finger (see Figure 1.1, p.4). Quite a lot of people do not have one of these, and that is good. It is rare, in any case, to have more than one or two, and where they occur it means that you are experiencing a time of restriction and difficulty in your life (Figure 9.2). If you know about your horoscope such a line will usually coincide with a difficult transit of Saturn in your chart.

However, as you will no doubt know by now, you can change this. Difficulties on your hands mean that you have allowed yourself to accept problems, that you have allowed yourself to think that you are at the mercy of events and,

worst of all, of 'fate'. You are not. Your mind is stronger
than any planetary magnetism that is supposed to affect you
psychologically and it is also stronger than difficult events
and circumstances that seem to pile up around you.

At first you may resist this idea because as children we
were of necessity kept under control by others. Unfortunately, as we grow to adulthood, elements of our childhood
powerlessness remain and can surface all through our lives to
thwart us. No one is to blame. It is simply the way parenting
and upbringing works. However, such difficulties resonate
with the Saturn energy so that we can end up succumbing to
apparent difficulties; and if we are to become fully functional
adults who are achieving our full potential, we have to root
them out.

Another important facet of Saturn is its image as Father
Time. The notion of limited time is a Saturnine one and in
fact in older myths Saturn was seen as the grim reaper and
associated with death. Since the idea of life and death is the
feeling of only having a limited amount of time to fulfil

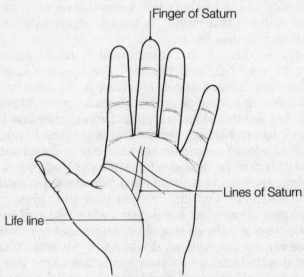

Figure 9.2

ourselves on this planet, exercises to soften your attitudes and extend your life will have a beneficial effect on your capacity to achieve what you want and to enjoy life.

Beginning to Understand Your Own Concept of Time

Time began for us as children when we began to understand the intervals between our meals, between getting up and going to bed, between our favourite TV programmes and so on.

At school this became a rigid structure and we had to be able to read a clock to 'tell the time'. When we learned to count, many of us created mental pictures of numbers and these became transferred to our images of certain ages. For example, in your counting books you may have had the pictures of two ducks swimming for the figure 2, of three boats sailing for the figure 3, four children playing for the figure 4, five kites flying for the figure 5, and so on.

Even at this early stage these images become linked with feelings as part of your visual repertoire so that your concept of twenty would have contained within it that first image of the ducks, for example, and the figure 2. This concept would also have become bound up with your feelings at that time – feelings such as whether the teacher liked you, or whether little Johnny had tripped you up in the playground, whether your parents were happy or miserable. The whole confused jumble of environmental influences – the sounds, the smells, the colours, the pictures as you are learning – become blended together along with your concept of particular numbers. Worst of all, you have probably forgotten all about it and don't understand why you feel the way you do.

Step 1

Take a pen and paper and write slowly the numbers from 1 to 10.

Do any of them strike you in any way? Do any of them give you a good feeling or bad feeling?

Quite a few people feel nothing in particular, but do try to unravel any connection. Did something happen at that age? If so, what, and how did it affect you?

I get a slight contraction at the figure 7 and I don't like the number. Everything seems dark around it. When I was seven we left the city to move to the country and for me the village school was almost unremittingly hostile. It was only at the age of 11, when I moved on to another school, that light seems to enter the figures. I still tend to see the figures of 7, 8, 9 and 10 as dark and I've just realised that I unconsciously avoid them when I'm picking lottery numbers; so it could be seriously upsetting my wealth!

If you have something like this, close your eyes, go back in your memory and see the situation in detail. Remind yourself that it is past and that you don't need its impression to last for ever. Consciously let it go, and if there are other people involved, release yourself from them. You can't change the past but you *can* change your mind about it. You can release the trauma of it where it still sits locked in your memory and in your cells.

Step 2

Write down all the tens – 10, 20, 30, 40, 50, 60, 70, 80, 90, 100.

Do any of these figures strike you in any way? You may get particular images or some may seem light or dark.

Step 3

Close your eyes and say the same figures mentally very slowly. Do any of them strike you now? Do any of them make you feel uneasy? Or lighthearted and free?

If you do notice differences try to remember when you were taught to count. You may simply have had difficulty getting as far as 30, tripping up on 28 or 29 for example;

or you may have felt tired or bored by the time you reached 40 or 50. Similarly, when you learned your tables, you may have had difficulty with things like $7 \times 8 = 56$ or $9 \times 9 = 81$.

The trouble is that whatever apparently small ideas or images you may have built into your concept of counting will also be reflected in your feelings about your age when you reach those figures. Completely daft, isn't it? But that's precisely the kind of connection the brain makes all the time, entangling your emotions with mental concepts.

The same is true of money. Some people can easily imagine having a capital sum of, say £3,000 or £4,000, but become panicky at the prospect of £60,000 or switch off completely at £600,000 and consequently upset their capacity to amass reasonable wealth. So look at your attitude to amounts of money in the same way as you did for figures in step 2. But this time put three zeros on the end of the numbers to represent thousands of pounds and see how these figures make you feel. If you become uneasy with certain figures, check them out as you did in step 3 and work on exercises to enhance good feelings about them.

So, if you have any dark or fatiguing feelings around certain figures, change them. Relearn your counting habits. Build in some fun. Just as you would have learned to count with pictures of two balloons, three horses, etc., build in new images that please you. Put in some of your goals perhaps, like pots of money, hearts and flowers. Make pictures of them with coloured pens or inks and brighten up your concepts.

Step 4

Look back at your list of figures in step 2 and now see them as ages. How does the age of 20 or 30 or 40 make you feel? Or 50, 60 or 70?

When we think about age we are drawing on the concepts of our culture. We are bombarded with them constantly; so to begin to break free of them, try transposing your feelings about them. If your feelings about 20 are light and free but about 40 are heavy and dark, switch the 20 feelings to 40. Fill the ages that seem dark with light.

Now, do you have a particular image about the age you are? Is it a good image? If so, excellent. If it's 'bad', do you actually *feel* bad about being this age? If so, stop it. Right this minute. This is an image you made up and it's affecting your life. Start to build in new ideas.

For example, let's suppose you're 38 and it feels OK but rather high up on your counting scale. It feels a bit grey, a bit near 40 and everyone says you're over the hill at 40. These days you're likely to live well beyond double that age. You're still young and full of vitality; so begin to see the decade ahead as one of ever-increasing life and enjoyment.

Do this for whatever age you are.

Step 5: Visualisation

Make yourself comfortable and close your eyes, breathing deeply and relaxing more on each breath. See the age you are now in figures. Whatever way it looks, brighten it up. You can also ask yourself if it needs some colour added to it. If a colour presents itself, use it. Allow the image to waft gently around your brain. This is a perfect age to be. You are alive and life is full of possibilities.

While still in this relaxed state you are going to undo some of the damage created by negative thinking. This damage has become structured in your physiology so that it becomes self-perpetuating.

Cast your mind back over the past year and make a mental note of the good things that have happened and how they made you feel. Recall also the difficult things. Both good and difficult situations have created stress in your system and you need to let it go. You can do this in two ways.

(a) Recall the event and breathe into it. Connect the inhale to the exhale as in Chapter 7 (page 137) for twenty breaths and remember the event in as much detail as you can. The increase of oxygen in the blood will help to lift the toxins from the cells and release them on the exhale.

(b) Recall the situation and see yourself as an observer of it. An observer usually has no emotional attachment so in this observing capacity release your own attachment to it. See what judgements and decisions you made about the situation and yourself and see whether this is what you want.

Decide what changes you would like in yourself and your life as a result of this and when you feel you have done enough you might like to write this down.

Step 6

Make a list of every year going backwards from your present age to your earliest memories. Write down the main events of each year – this can often require a bit of time so you don't need to do it all at once – and use it as a timetable to be dealt with chronologically, as in step 5, when you feel like it.

Some people make a commitment to do one or two sessions a week until they have covered their lives so far. In this way they begin to sort out why they have made certain choices and decisions about themselves and can rectify it for the future.

I first began to use this technique after the death of a close family member. I was deeply upset: I had moulded my life around this person's ideas and attitude to life. Because of the death, I realised that it was time to look at what I really wanted and where I was going. It was a powerful transformational tool.

Because of this person's views on money I had learned how to create wealth but my respect for the person had made me quite antagonistic and unsure of my femininity at times. This process enabled me to enhance my financial status even further and to become the basically laid-back wife and mother I had always wanted to be.

From that great trauma of bereavement I tracked back across my life, altering and adjusting everything so that I gradually uncovered who and what I really wanted to be.

I also used the technique to release ideas about death. Many people seem to start going downhill in their forties and fifties with negative ideas about dying, and it is those very ideas that are going to produce the results of illness and premature death. Techniques for overcoming the 'death urge' are outside the scope of this book but you will find more material in the Further Reading section.

Understanding and Overcoming Saturn in Your Life

Saturn is the planet of caution and discipline. In traditional astrology it presents us with difficulties to overcome and the way we handle these forms our character. But dealing with the difficulties that Saturn traditionally represents can also help you with your goals.

Working with Saturn

Give yourself an hour or two or even a morning for this exercise; and it is a good idea to plan it the night before. Because the effect of Saturn's energy is one of structure and form, you are going to structure your day.

If you go out to work you will be adhering to some kind of structure anyway, so it is best to do this exercise when you are free.

Step 1

Write out a detailed timetable for your morning. If you want to extend it to the afternoon, so much the better. Break down your time into at least half-hourly intervals, even if it is only to repeat the same activities preceding it. The idea is to impose structure and time on your day. Consider carefully the things you want to achieve in your morning and arrange them into your timetable.

Pin it up where you can see it.

Step 2

Follow your timetable to the letter, making a note of any-thing that took longer or less time than you had envisaged. Also note any resistance you had. You may suddenly feel that you want to branch out and do something else. Don't. But make a note of any feelings and especially any ideas you get.

Step 3

At the end of the session, take some paper and write down your goals for the next three months (you can tie this in with the goal-setting in Chapter 3 if you like).

Now divide this three months into the thirteen weeks it represents. You can use a calendar if you have one. Alternatively – and I tend to feel this is better – write headings of: week 1, week 2, week 3, etc., leaving a gap to write in.

Now, consider carefully what steps you need to take to achieve your three-month goals and put these in under each week.

For example, you may want to lose half a stone in weight and to improve your finances by £500. So divide half a stone (seven pounds) by 13, which will give you 0.538 pounds, which is the amount you need to lose each week in order to reach your goal.

Because your mind controls your body, if you are feeling joyous and positive and eating what your body tells you it needs, you will gradually lose weight anyway. Unfortunately, the majority of us have become 'stuck' and have lost touch with our bodies' wisdom.

These exercises will help to put you back in touch with

it. Furthermore, we are working here with the discipline of Saturn and dieting is actually a very Saturnine process. You need to cut out 3,500 calories to lose 1 pound; for our example that means cutting out 1,750 calories to lose 0.538 pounds in one week. So, for at least one week it is a good idea to experience calorie counting.

Similarly, for £500 you divide 500 by 13, which gives you about £38.50. This is the amount you need to achieve each week to reach your financial goal. You can then either work out ways, by saving or doing extra work, to create this amount or you can use the mind control techniques suggested in other chapters, especially Chapter 3.

The purpose here is not to give you the quickest or best way to achieve your goals, but to give you the experience of discipline and slog which, surprisingly, can often unlock a brilliant, creative idea within you, rather like a dam in a river where the water builds up and either breaks through the dam or diverts and finds a way round.

Step 4

Try to stay with this method of reaching your goals for at least a month before moving on to the next exercise.

Giving Saturn the Boot (1)

This exercise is similar to the one given under the Moon. There, you are acting on your first thought. Here, you are going to act on your feelings or gut instinct and if you decide to try the two approaches fairly close together, you will begin to understand yourself and the way your impulses and mind work much better. You will also discover which are the strategies that bring you success most quickly.

Step 1

Again, you need to give yourself a couple of hours or a

whole morning. Just as in the Moon exercise, go to bed the night before in as relaxed a state as possible. No late-night news or horror films.

When you wake up in the morning, do exactly what you feel like doing. Indulge yourself. Eat whatever you like for breakfast. Spend as long as you want in the shower or bath.

Now whereas with the Moon exercise you were to *act* on your first thought. This time on your first thought, ask yourself how it makes you *feel*. Would carrying out the thought make you feel happy? If so, do it. If it would make you uncomfortable, ask yourself what you would really like to do instead. You will probably see a significant connection between the first thought and the one that pleases you.

Everything you do during this morning must put you in a relaxed and happy frame of mind. So no adventures if the prospect worries you. No oughts, or shoulds or musts. Just relax and drift through the morning, pleasing yourself and make a note of each 'ought' thought that you don't really want to do: the essay or letter you don't really want to write. The visit to a relative you feel you ought to make but don't really want to do. Look at these later and decide what they are trying to tell you. Are there any changes you could make to your life? If certain things are permanently 'deadening' to you or lowering your energies, you must either change them or, at the very least, reduce their frequency in your life.

Step 2

At the end of your morning – or afternoon – again write down your goals for the next three months. You will already know the results of the previous goals exercise and now is the time to recall your feelings about this. You had to work on them; so how did it make you feel and how successful were you?

Now write down the following affirmations:

1. I——am successful in achieving all my goals whether I work at them or not.

2. I——easily achieve my goals by the power of my mind.

Write each of these at least six times each, noting down each time a negative thought or feeling comes up and create new affirmations around these. For example, you may feel, 'I got nowhere with my goals. It was boring and it pissed me off.'

Turn this into: 'I——now release the negative patterns I've built into achieving what I want. The more I set new goals the quicker I achieve them. I don't have time to get bored.'

Step 3

Write new goals for the next three months. Again divide them into a weekly structure but this time you:

1. simply read them each day;

2. write an appropriate affirmation out four or five times every day for a week or two if you can manage it.

You don't judge this. Above all you don't think 'Hell, it's the end of week three and I haven't even achieved week one. If such a thought arises, mentally or verbally affirm: 'This is a general timetable. My mind is achieving its goals even when I can't see it.'

Try to keep this up for at least a month. If you can manage the full three months, so much the better. Visualise your goals in as much detail as possible. Try to do this at least once a week.

When you want to give it a rest, just check which goal-setting technique worked the best for you and how it made you feel.

Both approaches are effective but in our society it is the first that tends to be paramount. Most of us have been trained in a saving mentality; so play around with the second approach as well and see what pleases you.

I use a combination of both and find that the second approach works best when I'm feeling buoyant and full of self-esteem. The first is good when I'm feeling dull and lethargic – the structure carries me through. However, the really huge improvements have tended to come with the second technique.

In Chapter 3 I explained how financially bogged down and struggling I had become and how in 1989 I decided to work seriously with all these techniques to get the life I really wanted. I mentioned there how successfully the processes worked; so about four years ago I decided to push myself even further. I was confident enough by then to know that the techniques worked and which ones worked best for me, so I decided to give up everything for three months and just write affirmations, visualise and do what I wanted, which often included meeting friends for lunch. The resulting expansion to my wealth and lifestyle was, without doubt, higher than ever before or since. Also, because I wasn't being stressed by work that I didn't want to do, I didn't need as much money to spend on things to 'escape' from stress.

I would get up at seven, get the family breakfast and see the children off to school. I would then take as long as I liked showering, washing my hair, deciding whether I would 'go with the flow' or whether I would be 'saturnine' and disciplined. Whatever approach I used, it had to feel right. The purpose was to contact my own energies and to use them to optimum effect and, above all, to enjoy it.

By 10 a.m. I was ready to sit down with a large mug of creamy filter coffee (I make no apologies to the health lobby – it's what I like and, therefore, part of the exercise). I had covered a plain folder with beautiful wrapping paper, and filled it with pastel-coloured lined A4 paper – and yes, you may laugh, as have a number of my friends who asked how twee could you get, but I happen to like writing on nice colours and so might you. Whatever works, use it.

I would then sit with my coffee and start to write affirmations in my folder. I would start with general ones to do with prosperity, health and beauty and allow the energy to move me forward so that the affirmations became more and more dynamic for me. I would never have shown my folder to anyone but since I hope you will find this technique useful for yourself as well I will admit that I started with basic things like:

1. 'I, Jacky, am now receiving large amounts of money from new and exciting sources' or:

2. 'I, Jacky, lose any excess weight easily and effortlessly.'

By the time I had come to the end I would be writing things like 'I, Jacky, am the most beautiful, exciting woman ever to walk the face of the earth and money flows to me in vast abundant amounts.'

I would be feeling as high as a kite, as if anything was possible – and that feeling is the one that produced the results. All sorts of things happened to improve my life but because I was in tune with my own energy, there was no strain. I would wake up with an idea for an investment and it would work out brilliantly. I would decide to treat myself to an expensive body lotion and discover that it was the day when the store was offering large discounts.

I would eat what I really wanted, and because my energy was high there was no hidden comfort need. The excess pounds just dropped off because my body was telling me what it needed. That could be bread and cakes and fruit one day. Steak and chips another. Seafood and wine another. Just whatever I really felt like.

To get back to the techniques which achieved all this, I would probably write affirmations for half an hour at coffee time.

At midday I often went out to meet a friend or group of friends for lunch. All were fascinated by my experiment and gradually all of them began to work in different ways with the techniques themselves. They all succeeded in some measure, and so can you. Anyone can do it. Absolutely anyone. You. Your mother. Your lover. Your best friend. Absolutely anyone. All you need is the desire to improve your life.

Anyway, after lunch my friends would go back to work and I would return home. At about 2 p.m. I would settle myself with a large mug of tea and my file to write a few more affirmations. Tea finished, I would then meditate and do visualisations for half an hour. It was during this period that I devised and began to use the techniques in this book, varying them each day depending on how I was feeling. I would finish by doing half an hour of yoga postures. There are some excellent videotapes on the market if you would like to try this too.

At 3.30 my children would be home from school and my only other session for the day might be a couple of minutes before I went to sleep, when I might program my mind to come up with some brilliant ideas for the next day.

Whenever I check back through my finances, some of the biggest gains I ever made were during this three-month period, and all my goals were achieved. So, if you feel like doing something like this, start off slowly with perhaps a week or two. If you have a job, don't throw it over unless you feel certain that it is time for a move and that you won't spend your free time worrying about whether the techniques work or not.

Remember, it had taken me three years from 1989 when I set the goal of not wanting to work all hours of the day and evening for a living before I was confident enough to let go and do this in 1992. During those first few years I was working spasmodically with the exercises – maybe half an hour a day for two weeks every three months or so. The achievement of the results I wanted gave me the confidence to go further.

Worry and doubt is the enemy of success. So work at your own pace and use the techniques when you *feel* you want to. You are your own boss, your own guru. Start having faith in your own ability to get what you want.

Working with Saturn in Daily Life

This exercise will also help to uncover habitual attitudes and assist you to achieve your goals.

Step 1

The Saturn energy is discipline, so spend a week living as frugally as you can. Buy the cheapest things in the supermarket, the cheapest brands, the special offers. Shop around to buy cheaper still. Save your carrier bags.

If you habitually use a car, use public transport.

If you usually eat out in restaurants, go to the fish and chip shop and eat out of a newspaper.

Look in skips and see if there's something you could use.

Look for clothes in second-hand shops or Oxfam or at jumble sales.

One friend got so hooked on this she not only continued for several months and saved a small fortune, she also began re-upholstering old furniture found in junk shops and skips, sold it, and bought a boat with the profits.

Step 2

You've probably guessed: you do the opposite of constraining yourself and let go. But you must keep within your means and limit yourself to a week. So, as far as your means will allow:

• Ride in taxis.

- Travel first class on trains.

- Buy the most expensive foods.

- Treat yourself to a meal at one of the expensive restaurants in town. Order the best.

- Look around at really expensive clothes. If your budget can stand it, buy something.

At the end of your week, compare the two ways of living. Most of us fall habitually somewhere between the two, but you now need to use both to achieve your goals.

Step 2 will have shown you the better side of life, so do your goals now need revision? You may want to incorporate more of this lifestyle into your calendar and as you do so your mind will become more creative at revealing and attracting new and better opportunities.

Equally, when you feel a bit down or a bit of a slump coming into your affairs, another stab at step 1 will quickly put more money in your pocket.

Giving Saturn the Boot (2)

Saturn is a serious energy. It has no sense of humour. Laughter is the best antidote to a touch of the Saturns. If you have a Saturn line anywhere on your life line, laughter at this time will not only help, it is a medicine.

Laughing physically massages our internal organs and releases feel-good endorphins into the bloodstream. Even smiling activates muscles and glands which lift the mood.

Keep a joke book

Whenever you hear a joke from a friend or on radio or TV, jot it down because you'll rarely remember it otherwise. Read the jokes over when you're feeling down.

Buy a book of jokes or limericks.

Make up your own limericks – you know the sort: 'There was an old woman from Ealing, Who had a peculiar feeling' . . . etc.

Invite friends to supper or a drink and make up communal limericks.

Play picture consequences. You know the ones where you draw a head and fold it over and pass it to your neighbour. You then draw neck and arms and fold it over and continue until you reach the feet. We played this with my mother one Christmas and she laughed so much that her tears washed out her contact lenses.

Use dice for options. Introduce chance into routine by writing out a list of six activities – three or four practical ones and two silly but non-harmful ones. Sally tried this on her stiff and rather Saturnine boyfriend of two months. Her six activities for a Sunday afternoon were:

- Watch TV.

- Go for a walk in the park.

- Go to Häagen-Dazs for ice-cream.

- Paint John's body with body paints.

- Collect weed from river for goldfish.

- Chat up the first person we see on the street.

John didn't like it but he allowed himself to be persuaded to throw the dice for two activities. It came up with collecting weed for the fish and having his body painted. He didn't fancy either option. It had begun to pour with rain and he preferred making love in the dark, not being spreadeagled stark naked to have his body painted.

Sally insisted; so they waded in torrential rain to collect the weed. John was grumbling all the time until Sally said she'd walk out of his life if he didn't shut up.

When they returned to John's house like drowned rats, she took his clothes off, dried him, laid him down and painted him all over. He was appalled. The more anguished he became, the more Sally laughed and told him he was too stuffy for words and she couldn't live with that.

He knew that he'd lose her if he didn't stop being so rigid, so he began to change.

His rigidity had come from his upbringing and living with Sally began to unravel it. They are married now and I can hardly believe he was ever as bad as she says he was. But she insists that all the exercises, of which the dice game was one, helped to unblock him, and the Saturn finger on his left hand began to straighten up from its former curve towards the finger of Sun which had indicated a conflict between creativity and upbringing.

Saturn and Health

Saturn is linked with the skeletal structure and the skin. All exercise will help to strengthen the bones, but the skin is often ignored.

Step 1

When you are doing one of the Saturn exercises for a week, decide to look after your skin.

Every day, brush it with a bristle hairbrush or bath-brush. Work from the feet up the legs, front, sides and back, upwards over the abdomen towards the heart. Brush upwards over the buttocks up and over the back towards the heart.

Brush downwards over the shoulders and arms.

This stimulates the nerve endings in the skin, the pores, and the lymph so that the skin can eliminate toxins.

Step 2

Moisturise your skin daily, applying the lotion and massaging it in the same direction as in step 1. You could also use essential oils, one or two drops per 10 millilitres of carrier oil such as almond or grapeseed. Lavender is generally therapeutic; advice from good stockists can be obtained from Culpeper's and Neal's Yard Apothecary (addresses in back).

Step 3

Stroke your skin lightly with your hands again in the same direction as steps 1 and 2. Use long, sweeping strokes. If you have a partner or friend to help you with this, so much the better.

Step 4

Close your eyes and contemplate your skin. Become aware of the way it covers every part of your structure, the way it is your contact with the outside world, the effect of warmth and cold, of water, of air, of the material of clothes. Imagine that the air you take in is being breathed out through your pores, as if your body is a whole breathing unit, centred around your lungs and heart. Everything you are is contained and connected by your skin.

Step 5

Saturn is associated with the earth element, so complement steps 1–4 by having a mud pack. You can buy mud packs from most chemists but the one I like best is Fango by Princess Marcella Borghese. You can get this from most good department stores and it is designed to be applied all over the body.

You will need an old bath towel so that you can cover yourself up after the application; and it is a good idea to go and lie down under a blanket or duvet for half an hour so that you can relax completely.

This isn't just for women. When I was buying some Fango a couple of years ago the assistant was in a flap because only half an hour earlier one of the Chippendales had come in and bought some, saying it was the best thing he knew to keep his skin in peak condition.

Step 6

Walk around your home stark naked for five minutes to allow the air to reach your skin. This can be at any time, not necessarily after a mud pack, but close the curtains if you don't want to upset the neighbours.

You will certainly begin to feel better, and with any or all of the exercises in this chapter, you will begin to notice a strengthening in the life line. Keep an eye on the other lines as well. Since Saturn tends to have a swamping effect on many areas of our lives, as you release its grip you may suddenly find that your head or heart line begins to strengthen or change direction.

10

Inspiration, Rejuvenation and Genius: Pluto, Neptune and Uranus

He who knows how to live can walk abroad without
fear . . . because he has no place for death to enter.
(Lao Tsu)

Neptune is the Roman god of the sea and is the planetary
ruler of Pisces, which is a water sign as you would expect.
It is associated with the spinal canal˚and is traditionally
regarded as a bridge between the conscious and unconscious
minds. The mount of Neptune is found at the base of the
hand near the wrist (Figure 10.1).

Although I have included the planets Pluto and Uranus
in this chapter, their relatively recent discovery has meant
that they have no placing in medieval palmistry. However,
the energies of Pluto and Uranus have been there all the time
and our hands reflect this. I have found that their natural
placing is next to the mount of Neptune at the base of the
palm near the wrist. It is a powerful energy and I will try
to simplify it for you.

Pluto is the ruler of Scorpio, co-ruling it with Mars. Many
of you will associate Pluto with the Roman god of the Underworld and the myth of Persephone, who was stolen by Pluto
and taken to the Underworld. Her distraught mother, in seeking to retrieve her, made a deal with Pluto so that Persephone
was allowed out after each winter. This story was used to
explain the rebirth of spring after the 'deadness' of winter.

In our own lives Pluto represents the deep, unconscious mind. We only use a tenth of our brain and the unconscious controls the other nine-tenths. It contains all our potential and all our fears and negative ideas; because it is unconscious, we rarely gain access to it, nor do we really know what power this potential and negativity is having over us.

Uranus, however, is associated with a tendency to break away from control. It represents the energy which gives rise to flashes of intuition and genius. We all have Uranus placed somewhere when we are born and it is there to help us to create new pathways and new ways of doing things. It is the essence of creativity, and the exercises in this chapter will help you to achieve your deepest goals.

The negative side of this energy is anarchy. Psychologically, this is revealed in deviant, fanatical and irresponsible behaviour. If you have this tendency – and you will certainly know if you have – all the exercises in this

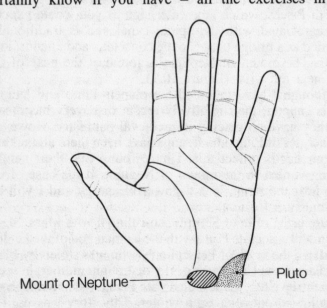

Mount of Neptune ——— Pluto

Figure 10.1

book will help to temper it so that your true creativity can blossom.

Uranus rules the zodiac sign of Aquarius. Many people already know that we will enter the Age of Aquarius in the early years of the twenty-first century. This will be a time of considerable upheaval and probably enormous creativity. By following these exercises you are putting your body and psyche into the most harmonious frame possible to make good use of these changes.

Whenever I have given deep techniques to people in order to contact these deeper, creative levels of the psyche, new lines have developed on this lower area of the hand next to Neptune.

If this area on your hand is full and well developed it means that you have a good deal of creative and intuitive potential. If you have lines – either fine or deep – travelling across it (Figure 10.2) it means that you are deeply imaginative and may possess some natural healing power. In this case, you probably also have a full mount of Neptune as well, so that the whole base of the palm looks full and rounded.

If these lines connect either to your life or head line on the *left* hand (Figures 10.2 and 10.3) it means that you will find fulfilment in healing and/or the creative arts. If you have this pattern on the right hand it means that you have already achieved, or will achieve, success in these areas. If you have this quality on the left hand and not on the right you need to work on it – maybe going to healing or creative arts workshops – and you will find new lines emerging on the right hand as well. Once a Pluto or Uranus line is connected to the head line so that it appears to be running parallel to the lifeline on the right hand, success is virtually assured. Nor do the lines take long to develop – anything from 2–3 weeks to a few months, depending on the level of your commitment.

The other really important factor about these two mounts is that they are associated with longevity. By accessing the energies that are represented by the mounts you can use

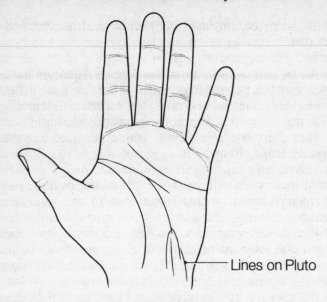

Lines on Pluto

Figure 10.2

them to enhance your life. Because the mounts of both Neptune and Pluto are situated at the base of the hand where the lifeline usually ends, I have come across some very unusual patterns in many people who have worked on improving their health, longevity and reversal of the ageing process.

Traditionally, a long life is indicated by the lifeline curving around the mount of Venus (Figure 10.3a). But in people who already have a long lifeline and have worked on these techniques, new lines have developed in *all* the cases I have seen. These have swung out into either the mount of Neptune or even wider into Pluto and Uranus (Figure 10.3b).

This could perhaps be explained by the lifeline needing the wider arc to express the increasing years of life – the wider arc gives it more space. However, all the people on whose hands I have seen this extension have been working on their health and Pluto/unconscious energies in themselves so that the wider arc through these areas is also expressing the fact that access to these parts of the psyche has been opened up.

As I have said before, your own mind is much more powerful than many outside forces, such as the planets which are often said to 'control' your life. It is for this reason that the lives of those strong-minded people who don't believe in astrology rarely follow the patterns that astrologers predict. Planets do not rule you: it is what you believe that rules you.

Most of us want to believe in good health and continuing vitality into old age. Some of us have also come to realise that age is a concept created by the mind. Research has shown that those people who meditate or practise yoga regularly have reversed or delayed the ageing process. As a result, they not only look as much as 25 – 30 years younger; their biological function is 25 – 30 years younger as well.

I will show you some additional exercises which will open your awareness of both Neptune and Pluto energies

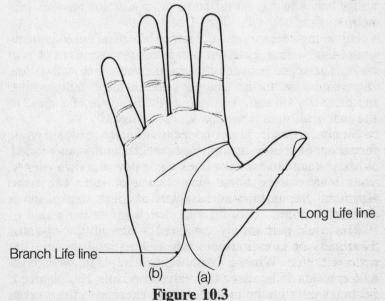

Figure 10.3

in your psyche and start you on the road to better health, longevity and continuing youthful looks. If you are older and feel that your face and body are beginning to crumple, these exercises will help you to turn the clock back. I mean it. You *can* reverse the ageing process. In fact, not only can – it is an absolute certainty once you have changed your belief systems.

Step 1: Contacting your essence

This title sounds grand but it is so simple and obvious that at first you may think it can have no effect.

Just find a few minutes when you can sit quietly and relax. You can stand up if you prefer. Now just breathe normally. It doesn't matter at this stage whether you breathe into the upper chest or the abdomen (see Chapter 7, p.137). Simply breathe in and out a few times in a relaxed way.

Now become aware of the space between your breaths. When you have breathed in, pause for a second or two and when you have breathed out, pause for another second or two.

Breathing keeps us alive. Each in-breath takes oxygen into your bloodstream. Each out-breath carries toxins out of your body. The space between breaths suspends this vital action. If we pause just for a second or two this major movement is momentarily slowed. You may become aware of a sense of the real you organising this whole process.

Breathe normally again, concentrating on the breath going in and out of your body until any other thought is suspended. What you are left with is pure awareness, your own energy, your own consciousness, your spiritual self. The word 'spiritual' has been bandied about so much that many of us have become confused and switch off at the sound of it. However, it is simply the essence of you, the essential awareness or consciousness when superficial thought has been removed. When it is unpolluted by negative thought and emotion it is also extremely powerful. The clearer it becomes through the practice of the exercises in this book, the healthier you will be. Begin to trust yourself and know that you can be what you want to be and have what you need and want.

Whenever the circumstances of your life appear difficult it is helpful to repeat the simple process above. It will help you to realise that the circumstances of your life are outside you. The real you is residing quietly *inside* and can feel serene whatever the situation. You can simply make a choice not to be upset by circumstances.

Gilly's Story

Gilly is a good example of what I mean. She was a 'consciousness junkie'. In other words, she was keen on spiritual growth and had tried many techniques but her parents, her father in particular, were deeply antagonistic to it all. Gilly was a bright, A-grade student, as were the rest of her family – brothers, sisters and cousins. Most of these did well, becoming bankers or starting successful businesses or marrying well. In her teens Gilly rejected all of it. She felt they were all misguided as she pursued her workshops, travelling to Europe, the US and India in the process.

When she was 30, Gilly married a man who taught workshops and whose main focus in life was spiritual growth, as Gilly's had always been. But money was not a priority for him, and now that she was married and her life had assumed the stamp of social respectability Gilly began to compare herself with her family. They were all wealthy, some with second homes in France and Spain, one with his own private aeroplane, and Gilly became dissatisfied.

I had known her for many years from workshops, and because I had a foot in both worlds – personal growth and an apparently respectable ordinary life – she asked me for help. Like most of us, the clarity Gilly needed was being obscured by her early upbringing. She had been surrounded by wealth, had turned away from it, and now it had become an issue for her. So wealth became Gilly's starting point: she set out creating more of it for herself and her husband. She set goals, she worked on affirmations, visualisation and all the other techniques outlined here.

When she started out, she had £5,000 in a building society account. Five years later she had £28,000. During this time she gave birth to three children and was not working, except to do the administrative work for her husband's workshops. The £28,000 was Gilly's own money created purely from the new ideas she conceived from her techniques. Like me, she discovered that the less she actually tried to make money in conventional ways like getting a job and the more she relied upon her inner goals and promptings, the more money she made.

However, she felt that £28,000 was peanuts in comparison with the wealth of her parents and siblings, and she became dissatisfied with her husband too, despite the fact that he was a loving partner and father. All her deepest issues came up and her father kept rubbing it in that she had not achieved her potential and could have married much better.

Better? This is a sign of cultural malaise. What is better than a loving family with enough money coming in, and, as Gilly had already proved, the ability to create as much as she needed?

At one point she became emotionally involved with another man – not to the point of going to bed with him but seriously enough to make her consider giving up her marriage. Only her love for her children stopped her.

I gave her all the body techniques in this book and she began to practise yoga regularly. All the while her children were growing up and all the while her husband was consistently loyal, loving and gentle and actually very successful.

The turning point came when her cousin, whose husband's business had turned him into a multi-millionaire, discovered that her husband had been having several affairs and these had started within three months of their marriage. Because of the money her cousin decided to stay with it, but Gilly realised that she had been envying a fantasy in her own mind, not the reality.

Along with her other techniques, she often included the exercise to contact her essence and would breathe steadily for ten minutes like this, pausing between each breath. As a result she began to understand that her own essence was the basis of her life and it had become very clear, free from negativity. Furthermore, freed from her bondage to her father's ideas, she had become much more gentle and feminine.

Step 2: Contacting deeper levels of your psyche

The following exercise is a visualisation to put you in touch with your unconscious self. You will probably find it helpful to tape this.

As with all the visualisation exercises, you need to find a time and place where you will be uninterrupted for fifteen to twenty minutes. Then breathe deeply into the abdomen, relaxing more with each breath.

When you feel you are as relaxed as you can be, imagine that you are walking in a wood where there is a special tree that has a door in its trunk. You go and find this tree, you open the door and discover steps that curve down deep into the ground. Take note of your surroundings as you begin to walk down the steps.

As you make your descent, there are several doorways leading away from the stairs. You choose one of these and open it.

What is the room like? Be aware of this as you walk to meet the guardian of this room. The guardian is coming to greet you and is an actual functioning part of your psyche. What does this person look like? Is it male or female? What characteristics does he/she have? You can ask the guardian anything you like. Do you need an answer about a relationship? Your work? Your finances? Ask the question that is uppermost in your mind and wait for an answer. An answer *will* come, even if it is in the form of a gift or appears vague at first.

When you have received this, you can either walk back up the stairs to the outer, conscious world, or you can ask to survey some other aspect of your psyche or body. You could look at health, for example, and as this chapter is about life and vitality I will take you further on this now.

Thank the guardian and either take him/her with you or return alone to the main stairway. One of the doors there is marked HEALTH so you go over to it, open it and make a note of how it looks. Some people see it like a large engine room, others see it like a relaxing health spa. You may see it very differently. This place has a guardian too and it is important to note how this person looks.

Ask to be shown a map of your body and its current state of health. This may be a computer or a chart or you may get an internal sense of how your health is. Imagine a large computer with your body illustrated on the screen. If there are any areas that seem depleted, see yourself pressing the right keys to delete this and overlay it with positive health. Imagine your computer with colours to key in as you like so that you can use cooling colours for inflammation and warm colours for sadness or low energies.

Now imagine that the computer screen enlarges your body map so that you go deeper and deeper into the muscles and bone right down to the cellular level. See the nuclei of the cells, and with your computer keys send energy to them to boost their vitality.

Now, move away from the screen and get an internal sense of yourself with these instructions actually taking place inside you. See energy being sent to each cell in every part of your body – your glands, your organs, your muscles, bones, skin and blood.

You are creating an actual physical effect. This process will actually improve your body.

When you feel you have done enough you can move away from here and go into another room if you want to. Perhaps you would like to look at your career or your love life. If so, thank the guardian and ask if there is anything he/she wants to say to you. When you feel ready, return to the main stairway.

Now go into the door marked CAREER and greet the guardian. Does this person have anything to tell you? You can then check your career in any way that appeals to you, but if you have no method in mind, you can either sit down with the guardian and go over your life together, or you can go to the computer and call up a chart of your career so far and look at possible changes and progress. This computer is special in that it can not only draw graphs and charts; it can also create pictures and images of possibilities. Press the keys to do this now and see what images come up. Don't worry if it all seems a bit vague: contact is being made and you may get an image more clearly later or when you wake up after a night's sleep.

You can do the same for your love life or relationships. Go back to the main staircase, enter the appropriate door and greet the guardian. Again you can sit down with this person and discuss your situation and/or you can go to the computer and log into it the things or people you want in your emotional life.

Take as much time as you need to fill in all the details. You may get a lovely feeling of being warm and nurtured or you may feel frustrated. Be easy with whatever comes up. The fact that you are making conscious contact with your subconscious is enough to initiate change.

Go into any door that represents part of your life and work with it in any way that pleases you or presents itself.

When you feel that you want to finish the session, thank the appropriate guardian and walk back up the stairs to the door which opens out into the wood.

Take a few deep breaths and slowly open your eyes.

At this stage it is a good idea to recall how your guardians looked. It can be quite a revelation and show you what to do next.

Eve's Story

Eve is in her late thirties, has been married since she was 19 and has three children aged 18, 16 and 15. She was beautiful, fashionable, and successful in her own mail-order business which she ran from home. To anyone who met her she had everything: a lovely home, lovely children, a loving husband, plenty of money and was completely organised – not a thing out of place and everything running like clockwork.

But she was dissatisfied. Something was missing and she decided to do this exercise.

The main guardian who greeted her was a witch doctor. He had big hair – a huge ball of black wiry fuzz – an animal skin around his waist for covering, and he kept dancing all round her.

The guardian for her health was a horse. It broke right out of the 'tree trunk' and started galloping across plains and beaches, its mane and tail flying free.

The guardian for her love life was a eunuch, huge and muscled but impotent.

All three of them represented part of her psyche, and when she surfaced from the exercise she saw immediately that the witch doctor represented a wild part of herself that was being suppressed. The horse represented her longing for liberation, to run away with no strings attached, while the eunuch told her how she saw her sex life. She loved her husband but their relationship had become stale.

Eve realised that she had been over-organised long enough and decided on radical change. She sold her business and left her family in the care of her mother for a month while she went to Italy to stay with friends who had an apartment in Florence. This holiday reinforced the change.

She decided to give herself time literally to 'reinvent her life', and since she wanted to give up her business she made plans and goals to enable her to live a more frugal lifestyle (see Chapters 3 and 9 for goal setting).

She said she had forgotten the joys of being able to play tennis and go swimming with the children or play board games with them. She took up embroidery and needlepoint, helping a friend who had an antique stall to restore the tapestry on stools and chairs.

She also had a torrid affair with a much younger man, which surprised her both by its intensity and how much it frightened her. She felt as if she were living on the edge of a precipice and realised not only how deeply she loved her husband but also that she needed him.

Like me, Eve decided that she had had enough of working so hard and juggling family life, and began to work on strategies to improve her financial situation without going back into business. She especially used the techniques in Chapters 3 and 9. It took her three years to build up a comfortable bank balance and to test the water with other work possibilities. She now gives lectures and writes on starting businesses from home for about four months of the year and, with a friend, has bought a second home by the sea for both their families to enjoy.

Like Eve you can reinvent your life as well but you don't have to be as radical as she was. You can work on your life piecemeal – change your work, reinvent your money and work towards becoming financially independent like Eve if you want to. Each step you make and each improvement that comes will reinforce your goals and clear your path.

The exercise on page 199 – 'Contacting Deeper Levels of Your Psyche' – is a good one to use whenever you feel stuck. It is quite normal for the 'guardian' to have changed his or her appearance and this will reflect the changes you have made in your life. These changes will also be reflected on your hands.

As you progress with these exercises, you will probably discover that other lines change on the hands before the Neptune/Pluto/Uranus axis does. You will probably see a strengthening and lengthening of the life line and sometimes a reddening of the line which means that the circulation is being stimulated there, paving the way to improved health and vitality. You may also see changes on the head line.

When lines start to appear on the Pluto mount, you are making very deep and powerful progress indeed.

11

Reinventing Your Life

By now you will have either read all through the book or dipped in here and there, or cheated entirely and turned straight here. Whatever you have done represents how you feel about initiating a new programme for yourself and is the best thing for you at the moment.

Before I suggest a good way for you to create an ongoing programme, I will just give you a few ideas with regard to your horoscope.

As you will know by now, your hands reflect the interaction of the planets when you were born but you will still probably want to keep looking at your 'stars' in magazines, and you can use the information in conjunction with this book. When you read that certain planets are transiting or that slow-moving planets like Saturn, Pluto and Uranus are changing signs, check the relevant chapters in this book and check your hands to see if they show any weakness or lack of development, so that you can work to improve it.

When you read any horoscope prediction, check your feelings about it. Does it make you feel happy? Uneasy? Or do you feel pessimistic?

The important thing to remember is that if the horoscope is predicting trouble, put it right out of your mind. The minute your mind begins to accept that trouble might lie ahead it will obligingly take it on board and make sure that trouble is what you will experience. Instead, work positively with the areas in which trouble has been predicted. If, for example, you have a prediction like one of mine recently which said that I was 'due for a date with financial destiny' and that it wouldn't be good, work on your financial goals, write affirmations, visualise, magnetise, and power-build. Don't let a negative prediction become self-fulfilling by believing it.

If the horoscope is predicting good things, then fine: work with that to enhance your life.

In both cases – a 'bad' or a 'good' prediction – go to the relevant chapters of this book and begin to work on some of the exercises and those from any other chapter if they appeal to you.

Once a Day

Ask yourself how you are feeling about your life or what you are doing. If you are dissatisfied, decide to do something to change it. Today, or at the very latest, tomorrow. It doesn't have to be something major. If you are fed up with work, take the day off and examine whether you are just temporarily bored or whether it is more serious. If the latter, you probably need to overhaul your job completely.

Similarly, with relationships. If, on a daily basis, you are continually unhappy, give yourself time to look at it – Chapter 7 will help – and decide to do something to help yourself forward.

Once a Week

Give yourself a treat. A cup of coffee at a favourite bistro or café, maybe? A meal? A long, luxurious soak in the bath? Whatever you choose, use the time to ask yourself how you feel. Happy and contented? Excellent. Your life is progressing on the right lines. Tense or worried? There is something for you to work on.

Whatever is bothering you, decide to work on it. If your love life is causing you grief, work on Chapters 6 and 7. The book suggestions in the appendix will give you further scope as well. Similarly, if money is your problem, read Chapters 3 and 9. Or if you feel generally dissatisfied, it is time to overhaul your blueprint. You can return to Chapter 2 and work through any other chapters relevant to your difficulties.

Every Three to Four Months

Make a note in your diary to remind you to do this: check how your life and plans are progressing.

It is quite usual for people to start the exercises and then tail off. Checking in regularly, but not too often, can boost you to get going again. Furthermore, your life will have progressed and some changes will have occurred; so it is a good time to reassess your direction and maybe focus on a particular aspect. The exercises on pages 176–180 are especially helpful here as they give two ways of working with three-month goals.

Once a Year around Your Birthday

This is a good time to do an overhaul of your life. How far have you achieved your goals? How far have you been successful? It is time to update your life.

Give yourself half an hour or so to sit down and check what has been achieved and then close your eyes to visualise what your ideal life would be like. It may have changed somewhat since your first exercises.

Before you finish this session, write out at least five things that you can do to move you towards the life you want. One of these things *must* be something you can implement right away or, at the very least, within a day or two. This will ensure that you are putting new energy into the next year.

Be vigilant at these annual check-ins. You will have moved on and your blueprint may no longer be as relevant. This is the time to sit down and create a new one. You will be experienced by now in recovering your childhood goals and dealing with difficulties, and it may be time to put that behind you. Your past will have been substantially cleared so that the future can open up with more vitality and opportunity for you.

You will be in a position to create totally different directions for yourself.

Finally

There will come a time when your life feels just right, possibly even wonderful. Your hands will also have changed to reflect this. For most people, improvements begin to take place within the first two or three months of working on these exercises and continue until that brilliant time when life is exactly as they want it. This usually takes somewhere between one and five years, depending on how much you focus on your goals and how much resistance you feel to having what you want.

One friend, a committed Christian, tied herself in knots for months because she had been taught to be humble and that poverty was preferable to wealth, and that she should accept her lot rather than attempt to change it. It was only when another friend reminded her that it was Christ himself who had said, 'Ask and you shall receive. Knock and the door will be opened unto you', that she decided to try the exercises.

Once the main resistance had gone, her life turned round in weeks. She went even further than these exercises and knelt down to pray, saying that she needed £5,000 to get a small complementary medicine business off the ground. Alongside these prayers, she felt impelled to give her services and skills in massage and reflexology free for several hours a week to a local hospice.

She did this for about two months, when she received considerably more than £5,000. It came as a gift from another church member who wrote to her saying that she had been struck by the radiant change in her and felt impelled to help her in her work.

So there you are. If you have big resistances as well, work on them, root them out and go for what you want. Everyone associated with you will be boosted by the change. Sometimes it can trigger their resistance as well and can lead to temporary friction as they sort themselves out. But that is actually a good sign. Also, like my friend, if you get a sudden 'hunch' to do something when you have been working on the exercises, or if you feel a warmth and rightness about a certain course of action, follow it through; it is your mind/body guiding you.

Above all, trust yourself and have fun working towards the life you really want. Enjoy the exercises and watch your life change. As you begin, it will appear to be something new that you are creating; but as you achieve it, you will realise that you are actually rediscovering who you really are: a more brilliant, more vibrant, more fulfilled you.

Further Reading

Chopra, Deepak, *Creating Affluence: Wealth Consciousness in the Field of Possibilities*, New World Library, 1993.

Gillies, Jerry, *Moneylove*, Warner Books, 1981.

Hay, Louise, *You Can Heal Your Life*, Eden Grove Editions, 1988.

James, Jacqueline, *Take Control of Your Life*, Hodder and Stoughton, 1995.

Laut, Phil, *Money Is My Friend*, Vivation Publishing, 1990.

Mayo, Jeff, *Teach Yourself Astrology*, Hodder and Stoughton, 1994.

Price, Shirley, *Practical Aromatherapy*, Thorsons, 1994.

Ray, Sondra, *The Only Diet There Is*, Celestial Arts, 1982.

Ray, Sondra, *I Deserve Love: The Secrets of a Great Relationship*, Celestial Arts, 1993.

Ray, Sondra and Orr, Leonard, *Rebirthing in the New Age*, Celestial Arts, 1993.

Sivananda Yoga Vedanta Centre, *Learn Yoga in a Weekend*, Dorling Kindersley, 1993.

Wilde, Stuart, *Miracles*, White Dove International, 1987.

Useful Addresses

Culpeper Ltd (essential oils, herbal remedies)
21 Bruton Street
Berkeley Square
London
Tel: 0171 629 4559

Neal's Yard Apothecary
5 Golden Cross Walk
Cornmarket Street
Oxford
Tel: 01865 245436

Rebirthing (general enquiries):

Gilly Montgomery
5 Manor Road, Catcott
Bridgwater
Somerset TA7 9HT
Tel: 01278 722536

Bookshops

Mysteries
9–11 Monmouth Street
London WC2N 4EZ
Tel: 0171 240 3688

Watkins Books Ltd
19 Cecil Court
London WC2N 4EZ
Tel: 0171 836 2182

The Inner Bookshop
111 Magdalen Road
Oxford
Tel: 01865 245301